Adopting
A Great Dog

NONA KILGORE BAUER

T.F.H. Publications, Inc.
One TFH Plaza
Third and Union Avenues
Neptune City, NJ 07753

This book has been published with the intent to provide accurate and authoritative information in regard to the subject matter within. While every precaution has been taken in preparation of this book, the publisher and author assume no responsibility for errors or omissions. Neither is any liability assumed for damages resulting from the use of the information herein.

ISBN: 0-7938-0533-3

Printed and bound in USA

www.tfh.com

Contents

. . . .

1

Shelter and Rescue Dogs: Who Are They?

· ·

We first saw him rummaging about in our front bushes, a long-legged yellow Lab eagerly sniffing the tantalizing dog smells deposited by our family of Golden Retrievers. We watched him snuffle every twig or stick that had been walked on, chewed, or anointed. Finally, satisfied with his shrubbery inspection, he trotted up to our front door and just stood there, furiously wagging his tail, waiting to be invited in.

Here was a dog that obviously was accustomed to spending time in a house. Dogs who live most of their life outside in a yard or dog pen (it shouldn't happen, but it does) don't know about front or back doors, nor would they expect to be allowed inside.

After an eternity of two or three minutes, the dog made no attempt to toddle off back to a master who was nowhere to be seen. The blacktop road near our farm is like many rural highways, a popular dumping ground for dogs. It's not uncommon to see stray dogs traveling alone or with a canine buddy, looking for a handout or a safe place to rest. The yellow dog had found such a place. Of course we took him in.

He wore no collar, and his fur showed no signs of having worn one. He was clean and in good shape, with no battle scars, so he hadn't been "on the road" very long. We called him simply "Yellow Dog," and he easily settled into our family dog routine. He was a real sugarplum who loved hugging more than eating and would leave his food pan to get his ears scratched at every opportunity.

We spent the next two weeks searching for his owner, calling our neighbors, and checking with the animal warden of our small town, with no luck.

Does this story have a happy ending? The good news is that in this part of the Midwest, Labradors are good candidates for adoption, and a humane society 50 miles away agreed to help find a home for Yellow Dog. Three weeks later, he was bouncing

There are many reasons why dogs are given up or abandoned. The lucky ones are adopted into loving homes.

around in a new backyard, playing with six kids who thought he was the very best dog they ever owned.

The bad news is that Yellow Dog is one of the lucky ones, one of that small percentage of stray and abandoned dogs who find a happy home. Most strays end up euthanized because there are too many dogs and too few people willing to adopt them.

Abandoned Dogs: Some Reasons

Shelters and breed rescue organizations can rattle off a long list of reasons why owners give up their dogs. Many are frivolous, a few of them legitimate, but none would happen at all if people thought more about the animals before they got them in the first place. Sadly, the most common reasons for dog abandonment are the fault of the owner, not the dog. Here are some of the more common reasons owners offer when turning in their dog.

Behavior Problems

More dogs are taken to shelters for bad or inappropriate behavior than for any other reason. An estimated 7.5 million pets enter animal shelters each year, many turned in by their owners for behavior problems. A study by the Morris Animal Foundation found that behavioral problems were the leading cause of death in dogs. "He barks too much," "chews too much," "digs in the flower bed," "jumps on the kids," "guards his food dish," - the list goes on and on. In 1996, one veterinary journal reported that 50 percent of puppies who were adopted or purchased would not be in their original homes one year later. Three-quarters of those pups would be abandoned because the puppy "misbehaved." The study observed that those puppies that end up in shelters or dumped along the road have little prospect of getting a second chance in life. Backup statistics from the American Society for the Prevention of Cruelty to Animals state that 80 percent of household pets in the United States will not die in their first home.

Although many dogs are given up because of unacceptable behavior, most problems are preventable with basic training.

Most behavior problems are preventable. Bad behaviors occur because the owner didn't take the time to train the dog or didn't understand the dog's natural behaviors or how to communicate in canine terms. Don't let that happen to you and your new companion.

Before you decide to adopt a dog, be certain you will have enough time to exercise, train, and play with him. Dogs are social creatures and need to feel loved and wanted. They also need to be taught how to behave using gentle, but firm and consistent, guidance.

Time Constraints

Some owners surrender well-behaved dogs simply because the family has developed other interests and no longer has time to tend the dog, or they never had enough time to begin with and didn't realize it. In the typical family, the kids are into sports, mom gets a new job, or everyone's too busy or too tired. The dog is always in the way. It speaks well of the dog who lives through such neglect without developing serious behavior problems. Such dogs offer great adoption potential. When adopted, they are usually so grateful for love and attention from their new owner that they adjust quickly to their new environment and family structure.

Life Circumstances

The most tragic reason for surrender is the death of the owner. Suddenly, a dog who is loved and cared for is left homeless because his owner dies. Most people fail to consider what will happen to their pet in the event of their death or the death of their spouse. Sometimes the surviving spouse is unable or unwilling to care for the dog.

All dog owners should include their pet(s) in the provisions of their will or state their wishes in writing as to the disposition of the dog in the event of death. Be sure a family member or a friend is willing to care for the dog or agrees to place it in a new and loving home.

Divorce spells the same heartache for the dog. It's "his" or "hers," and often the dog has to go. The dog didn't cause any problems, but suddenly becomes one.

Usually, adopted dogs are so grateful for love and attention that they quickly adjust to their new family.

Dogs who are the victims of death or divorce are usually well-behaved pets who will gladly offer their allegiance to a new owner, given a reasonable adjustment period. The dog won't understand why he's suddenly "homeless" and may be cautious or suspicious of his new surroundings. This situation requires time, patience and loving care—occasionally more time than you expect—but it will be worth it.

Wrong Choice

Too many dogs are surrendered because the owners made the wrong decision in the breed they chose. They selected a breed because it was "cute," "big," "small," or "cuddly," without researching the character and personality of the dog or its needs. Is it easy to train, good with kids, easy to groom? They never knew that adorable puppy would be 80 pounds at nine months old! They didn't understand this is a high-energy dog who needs lots of exercise; nor did they imagine dog hair on their white carpeting or the time involved in grooming the dog's lush fur coat.

It's hard to resist taking that adorable puppy home, but before you do, make sure that everyone concerned is able and willing to take care of a dog.

Impulse Puppies

Very often a puppy joins the family as an "impulse purchase." The Christmas puppy for the grand-children, the little fluffball in the pet shop window, an irresistible puppy leftover from the litter down the street: These are all puppies who don't

You may not know the background of your adopted dog, but with patience and understanding, he can become a member of your family.

work out because of people who didn't use common dog sense to begin with.

Animal Cruelty

Animal cruelty is against the law; in some states it's a felony, but the law still can't protect many dogs from abuse, neglect, and often unspeakable cruelty at the hands of their owners. Breed rescue organizations often rescue large numbers of dogs from despicable conditions: dogs tied up and starving; dogs tortured, burned, used for fighting or as bait for fighting dogs; dogs booted out of cars speeding along the highway. Frequently, many of the rescued animals are beyond help and must be destroyed. The salvageable survivors go into foster care, where they are evaluated and eventually adopted. Many will require long-term rehabilitation with an adoptive family who is willing to go the extra mile in the three P's: Praise, Patience, and Persistence.

Strays

The majority of dogs at shelters are strays who come in through animal control or are brought in by citizens who find them wandering in backyards, scavenging in empty lots, or running loose along the road. It's not uncommon for shelter personnel to arrive at work and find a box of puppies sitting at the front door or a sad and frightened dog tied to the gate with no note or explanation. These dogs all arrive with question marks about the dog's temperament, health, and history.

The fact is that many of these discarded dogs are simply victims, good fellows who will make great pets once they are rehomed with a family who understands the needs of the individual dog and is committed to caring for the animal for his entire lifetime. The dog you adopt today can and will be as special as the dog you adored when you were growing up, as loving as the dog who shared your life for the past decade or two, even as exceptional as the dog you fantasized about owning and never could, until now.

2

Should You Adopt a Dog?
. . . .

Certainly, there are many joys associated with dog ownership, and knowing that you've come to the rescue may make bringing home a shelter dog even sweeter. Yes, there are many advantages to adopting, but the responsibilities that follow are the same as owning any dog—time, energy, money, love, and dedication. For the sake of any dog you're considering as a companion, you should take some extra time to think ahead.

Benefits of Adopting

So why should you adopt a dog from a shelter or rescue group? Why not buy a pup from a breeder or a neighbor who plans to have puppies sometime soon? Most people who adopt their pets do so because they feel they're contributing to the war against pet overpopulation by saving a dog from euthanasia. One shelter statistic reveals that each year a shelter dog is euthanized every 6.7 seconds. That's not surprising when another statistic estimates that in the United States over 2,000 puppies are born every hour, compared with 415 human beings.

Dogs of All Ages

If you're concerned about finding a shelter filled with mostly

An older dog can make the perfect pet for the right household.

older dogs, shelter figures also show that over 75 percent of adopted shelter dogs are younger than six months of age and that only 16 percent of dogs are over one year old when acquired. Good news for those looking for a young dog.

Cost

Another obvious advantage of adoption is the initial cost. Although adoption fees vary, the cost is still less than the purchase of a purebred pup. Most of the older dogs often have updated shots and may already be spayed or neutered, while puppies will need a complete battery of shots and early veterinary care. However, don't confuse the reduced initial cost with the lifetime expense of owning the dog.

Should You Own a Dog?

While you're debating your decision to adopt, you should also

Shelter Advocates

Ask anyone who has adopted a dog from a rescue or shelter, and they'll agree: "This is the best dog we ever had," "the best thing we ever did," "he's like one of our children," "we were made for each other." If you're thinking "new dog" and you've never visited a shelter, now's the time. You'll be amazed at the many fine dogs who are housed there. Most of them have the potential to become a sterling member of a family that is properly matched to their size and personality.

Dogs who have been abandoned or mistreated usually bond eagerly with humans who offer them attention and loving care. It may take a while, especially with dogs who have been abused, but your rehabilitated dog will love you unconditionally for life, which is the ultimate bonus of owning a dog.

examine the reasons why you want a dog in the first place and what kind of dog you're looking for. You want to be sure your dog doesn't end up back at the shelter because you led with your heart and not your head. There are important questions to ask – and honestly answer – before making the commitment to adopt a dog.

Time

Will a dog fit into your busy schedule; do you have enough time? This is one of the major reasons owners give up their pets, and for the animal's sake, you don't want history to repeat itself. Most breeds, or combinations of breeds, have different exercise requirements, and some need plenty of heavy-duty playtime or they will redirect their energy into creative mischief. You must allow lots of time to exercise your dog, take him to obedience class, teach him basic house manners, then make sure you have the time to maintain those courtesies. (Yes, dogs need routine reminders and reinforcement just like children do. It's like living with a five-year-old for life.)

Space

Will your living quarters best accommodate a large or small animal? A large dog requires more space and should have a fenced backyard. Small dogs are more popular and more acceptable in apartments or condominiums. If you rent or live in a multiple-family dwelling, be sure you have written permission to bring a dog into your building or complex and that you understand any restrictions that apply, special potty and exercise areas or times, and poop-scooping rules (a must if your dog is to remain welcome).

Budget

Can you afford to own a dog? Like children, dogs need more than love. Food, veterinary care, training classes, registration fees, grooming, miscellaneous items, and probable pest control make up a hefty canine expense account. Based on an 11-year lifespan, and depending on the animal's size ("large" dogs cost more to feed and outfit), the average dog will cost at least a few hundred dollars a year for food, plus medical attention and grooming if you own a breed that may require professional care: This totals up to tens of thousands during his lifetime. And that doesn't include the initial cost of the dog. If your budget is already stretched, maybe you should reconsider.

Before you take a dog home from the shelter, make sure you have a safe area in which he can play and exercise.

Dog Hair

Will dog hair drive you crazy? Most dogs shed, some more than others. Certain long-haired breeds require extra time for extensive grooming to keep their long coats free of mats and tangles. (When a heavy or double-coated breed sheds its winter coat, you'll wear out your brushing arm.) Will you have time to do it? Can you afford a groomer? If dog hair is unacceptable, consider a non-shedding breed. However, those few dogs who don't shed must be groomed regularly or their coats become seriously matted, so be sure you can afford professional services for coat care.

Depending on the breed or mix of breeds, some adopted dogs need more coat care than others. The time and cost of grooming should be considered before taking a dog home.

3

Shelter and Rescue Organizations

. . . .

Across the United States stretches a vast network of animal shelters and rescue groups that are dedicated to saving and rehoming unwanted pets. The people who volunteer and work for these organizations are caring and compassionate animal lovers; they have to be. Only a strong love for animals could sustain the dedication needed under such stressful conditions. Every day they care for frightened dogs brought in by animal control and accept unwanted companions from owners. Every week many are forced to euthanize dogs because there's not enough room, time, money, or willing adopters to save them all. Their greatest satisfaction is placing a dog in a permanent home with people who will love the dog forever.

Animal Shelters

Most animal shelters operate as independent agencies. Some fall under city or county jurisdiction and operate with local tax funds. City shelters are usually staffed by local government employees. Some municipalities handle animal control through non-profit humane societies that often depend on charitable donations. Humane societies are managed by their own independent board of directors and rely heavily on volunteers and contributions.

Animal shelters and humane societies are two reputable places to find a canine companion.

While the operating policies of each agency vary according to state and local laws and, of course, available funds, most shelters share the common goal of finding compatible homes for as many dogs as possible. Most require spaying/neutering as a condition of adoption and offer the surgery at special rates or as part of the adoption fee.

Some animal shelters work in cooperation with the larger pet supply outlets to host "adoption days." Check local newspapers for these weekend events or visit your nearest pet superstore.

Humane Societies

Humane societies also offer animals for adoption but often provide additional services to the pet community. Some offer pet-assisted therapy programs to area hospitals and nursing homes where volunteers take puppies, kittens, and other good-natured animals on weekly visits to those institutions. Others offer discounts on obedience classes and free adoptions to senior citizens. Many shelters and humane societies work with local breed rescue volunteers when a dog of their chosen breed is unclaimed and might face euthanasia.

Neither private nor public shelters are governed by any of the well-known national humane organizations. The Humane Society

Some shelters will offer veterinary care, temperament testing, and training classes to the dogs in their care in order to better place them in suitable homes.

of the United States (HSUS) is a nonprofit organization that promotes education to foster the humane treatment of animals. The American Humane Association (AHA) is also nonprofit and was founded in 1877 to prevent cruelty and neglect to both children and animals. The American Society of the Prevention of Cruelty to Animals (ASPCA) is the headquarters for national humane education programs and has been the official shelter for New York City since 1866. (For more information on these and other organizations, see the Resources section.)

According to the Humane Society of the United States, for every loved and cared-for dog and cat there are nine others that are homeless, in shelters or roaming the street. An estimated 25 percent of these creatures are purebred dogs.

Humane Society of Missouri

Founded in 1870, Humane Society of Missouri is the fourth-largest and fifth-oldest humane society in the United States. As a not-for-profit corporation, they provide services and programs to the community without local, state, or federal tax support.

This Humane Society has witnessed some changes in the canine population over the past few years: purebred dogs are now about 40 percent, up from the customary 25 percent. Most purebred owner turn-ins arrive at about three months old, with behavior problems as the most commonly cited reason.

When a dog is accepted into the center, it's placed on a 24-hour hold, then goes through a health and temperament screening process and becomes available for adoption. Strays arrive through animal control or other sources, are held five days, examined on day six, then held for 24 hours and turned into the general adoption population. All dogs accepted receive the necessary shots and are tested for heartworm and other internal parasites, and flea-dipped if necessary.

When clients first come to the center to adopt a dog, they go through the dog rooms—one for puppies, and one each for adult males and females. If they decide on a dog or puppy, they take the animal into the get-acquainted room to visit and complete the adoption questionnaire.

Certain questions are designed as "red flags" to warn the staff to look more closely at the client and the care the animal will receive. The staff always prefers to educate and work with the client. The staff also does some puppy testing and subordination exercises, especially if the client has young children. If the client refuses to cooperate, he will be denied a dog. In some cases, the staff requires proof that a fence has been erected or will send an investigator to the home before releasing an animal to a questionable situation.

With strict adoption criteria, the return rate on dogs is less than 10 percent.

Breed Rescue

In 2003, the American Kennel Club (AKC) had a record of approximately 276 breed rescues in the United States. That triple-digit number is one more sad commentary on the fate of purebred dogs in today's society. The following are but a few examples of the rescues that exist in our country today. You can find a rescue contact for whatever breed you've interested in by going to www.akc.org and searching for breed rescue.

Greyhound Rescue and Adoption

Greyhound rescue is by far the largest purebred adoption operation in the United States. There are about 30 of these ex-racing groups in the United States. Many are local groups who operate within a small geographic region. Others have several chapters nationwide and can refer interested parties to the

Shelter workers spend a lot of time with each dog so that they can match it with the appropriate owner.

nearest chapter. Cindy Cash is one of several Greyhound devotees who coordinate Greyhound adoptions across the United States. Whenever a Greyhound racetrack closes permanently or temporarily for the season, Cindy pairs the "retired" racing dogs with adoption groups, then enlists professional haulers who drive the dogs to new locations for foster home placement or adoption.

These Greyhound "hauls" often take the drivers (always teams of two) thousands of miles across many state lines, with drop sites from Texas or Florida through Oklahoma, Missouri, Indiana, and beyond into the East Coast or western states. It's not uncommon for 50 to 75 Greyhounds to travel en masse, with specific groups of dogs delivered to adoption groups at specific drop-off points.

Ex-racing Greyhounds make gentle and loving pets, and Greyhound rescue is one of the largest rescue organizations in the US.

Like many haul coordinators, Cindy tries to move the dogs to metropolitan areas such as Chicago where there are no Greyhound tracks and therefore greater adoption potential. (About 35 percent of all Greyhound racers are in the state of Florida.) She also tries to divide the dogs by sex and color so each rescue location will receive a variety of dogs to place. Cindy tries to profile the dogs who will be arriving to give the rescue groups some idea of what kind will be available. She also works hard to fill specific needs, as when a rescue group has an adoption request for a "quiet black male" or a "smaller brindle female."

Sandy Snyman is one of Cindy's haulers and is best known as "Greyhound Granny." At almost 60 years old, Sandy drives 100,000 miles cross-country every year delivering retired Greyhounds to be rehomed through rescue groups. Sandy works closely with Cindy to plan her routes and destinations whenever dogs become available.

Sandy runs the Greyhound adoption center for Greyhound Pets of America at the Daytona Beach Kennel Club Racetrack. Her adoptions are not limited to only GPA rescues, however, and she takes Greyhounds in from anywhere and everywhere, including other racetracks and the local humane society.

When Sandy hits the road with her Greyhounds, every dog already has a home or an adoption group ready to accept the dog. Each dog has been spayed or neutered, has had its shots and heartworm check, has been wormed for parasites, and has had its teeth cleaned and fluoride treated.

Quincy, Illinois veterinarian Joanne Klingele and her Racers Recycled rescue operation is frequently on Sandy's rescue route. Over a four-year period, Joanne has accepted over 70 Greyhounds from Cindy Cash, Greyhound Granny, and other Greyhound adoption groups who had dogs who desperately needed placement. Joanne performs a complete veterinary work-up on each dog, completes their shots, heartworm and parasite testing, spays or neuters, and cleans their teeth. She socializes the dogs and evaluates each personality to match them appropriately with their new adoptive families. Occasionally, she keeps one or more for longer-term rehabilitation before they go into their new homes.

Golden Retriever Rescue

The Golden Retriever Club of America has over 30 active rescue groups that work within their member club network. These dedicated Golden lovers annually rescue thousands of Goldens from animal shelters, owner turn-ins, and random pick-ups from the streets and other sources. Like most breed rescue folks, these people dig deep into their personal time and often their pocketbooks, working for the welfare and betterment of the breed they so love.

A rescue is an association, run buy breed enthusiasts, that fosters purebred dogs and helps to find them a good home.

Akita Rescue

Nancy Baun of Hawthorne, New Jersey, heads up ARMAC, the Akita Rescue Mid-Atlantic Coast, Inc., for the Akita Club of America. ARMAC is quite blunt in their rescue statement that "Akitas are not for everyone!" A 44-page rescue packet provides detailed information about the breed and protectively emphasizes the negative side, i.e., that this noble breed is extremely dominant and if you fail the dog's first challenge, you will not wish to live with him. These cuddly teddy-bear puppies grow rapidly into aggressive adults who are still used in Japan to hunt bear and wild boar. Akita Rescue urges potential owners to seriously research the breed to prevent another Akita ending up as a shelter or rescue statistic.

Rottweiler Rescue

In the last decade, Rottweilers numbered in the top five most popular breeds registered with the AKC. Such popularity is never good news for any

Breeds like the Rottweiler are popular, but they are not for everybody. Rescues help match them with the best owners and living situations.

breed, since it leads to indiscriminate breeding and breed deterioration. As a large, imposing, guarding breed, Rottweilers have suffered at the hands of unscrupulous breeders and buyers. Rescue volunteers routinely rescue Rottweilers from horrific situations. The fact that so many of these gentle giants rehome successfully is testimony to their loving and tenacious spirit.

A Few Good Folks and Dogs

Unfortunately, too few people seek the services of rescue groups or even shelters. It's easier to dump their dog along a rural highway, drop him off at an interstate rest area, or leave him tied to a tree in the park. Many of the people who abandon their dogs for frivolous or irresponsible reasons don't want to confront their guilt or admit their failure to the shelter or the rescue person—it's easier to hope or pretend someone will find the dog.

Many dogs are relinquished to shelters or rescues during puppyhood and adolescence because owners do not understand that training, time, and guidance can remedy most problems.

However, not all people who relinquish their dogs are callous or unfeeling. Unexpected changes may force a family to give up a beloved dog. Children become allergic to dog dander, a parent falls seriously ill, loses his or her job, or is transferred overseas where there is a six-month quarantine on dogs. These dogs are usually ideal candidates for adoption. Most shelters try their level best to evaluate every dog admitted to determine its potential for adoption. Their efforts depend on the time and money available, so some shelters have the luxury of interacting more frequently or intimately with their canine charges. The amount and quality of the time they spend with the dogs determines what kind of opinion they can offer on their disposition and behavior. Many shelters will hold a dog beyond the required holding period depending on the dog's health, disposition, and how the dog presents itself to the public.

Dog Adoption Goes High-Tech

Pets have become a major presence on the information superhighway with the arrival of a proliferation of internet resources for people who are considering pet adoption. Many breed clubs, rescue organizations, humane societies, and animal shelters have websites that give information about the organizations and descriptions of the pets that are available for adoption. These sites are updated regularly, some even daily, to stay current. The amount of information out there can be somewhat overwhelming, so it's best to have time and patience when "surfing the 'net" for a pet. Some options are presented here, and you will also findweb sites for orginizations listed in the Resource section.

If you have a specific breed in mind, the national breed club's site will provide you with breed rescue information or a link to the

Most shelters try their best to evaluate each dog to determine its potential for adoption.

There are many resources available, including websites, which can help you locate and adopt the right dog for you.

breed rescue's site. You can access the national club or the breed rescue directly if you know their web address; if you do not, enter the breed's name into the search engine to generate a link through which you can directly access the club's home page. If the national breed club is not online, you should still be able to find some type of regional or local organization. Searching for a specific breed will also generate a list of related sites, one of which may link you directly to the breed rescue. Also, the AKC has a website that contains a list of breed rescues.

If you are looking for shelters and humane societies in your area, searching for "pets and adoption," "SPCA," "humane society," or a related term will generate a list of shelters and pet adoption agencies that have websites, and you can access whichever ones interest you.

There are also online pet "locator" services that will search their databases for a particular type of dog (or other type of pet) according to the criteria that you input. If there are any dogs that meet your criteria, these services will give you the locations where this type of dog is available for adoption.

You may be able to find some information by checking the dog-related chat rooms and message boards on the online service that you use. Some people use the message boards as "classifieds" to list dogs that need new homes, and the dog lovers that you can meet in chat rooms may be able to share some valuable advice with you.

Whatever you choose, you will find that many of these online resources are not just informative, but fun. In addition to dog adoption information, some also offer pet-related merchandise, give information about boarding kennels and grooming, invite visitors to share their pet adoption stories, etc. The possibilities are almost endless, and who knows—you may end up with a new four-legged friend.

4

What Kind of Dog Should
You Adopt?

· · · · · · · · · · · · · · · · · · ·

A visit to a shelter can be somewhat overwhelming, given the number of needy and worthy dogs waiting to be adopted. To help you deal with a potentially emotional decision-making process, there are several important issues to consider. What kind of dog is right for you? For your family? For your lifestyle? Do you have time to train a puppy? Do you have your heart set on a particular breed? All these questions should be answered before making a final decision.

Companion Dog

Do you want a family companion for your children or an aging parent? If your kids are active or rambunctious, always climbing trees and playing tag football, consider a dog or breed that would happily join such activities without being intimidated or easily hurt. A shy or quiet child might be happier with a smaller or less active dog. An elderly person may prefer a couch-potato pooch that is willing to lounge in front of the TV much of the day. Are you a hunter, a sailor, a hiker? Do you jog and dream of four furry feet running at your side? What about dog shows or other forms of canine competition—do you want get involved in these?

Your lifestyle and interests should factor in your decision to adopt and what kind of dog you choose.

Your lifestyle and interests are an important barometer in your decision to adopt a dog and what type or breed you choose.

Watchdog

Are you looking for a watchdog or a guard dog who will make you feel safe and more secure? Most dogs can be trained to bark at a strange noise or signal the approach of a stranger or intruder. However, adopting a large breed known for its aggressive tendencies would present serious training problems for the average or novice dog owner. Few people are experienced enough to train or control a dog who is naturally prone to be defensive with strangers. Without expert control, such an animal also could threaten the safety of your own family and friends. Further, many popular guard dog breeds are at the shelter because their owners failed to train them properly and were unable to control them. Reversing those tendencies could be difficult to impossible, and such aggressiveness should be dealt with only by professionals who have experience in attack and guard dog training.

The Older Dog

When you adopt a dog who has grown beyond the cute puppy stage, what you see is what you get. This dog will not surprise you by growing up and up, beyond your wildest dreams. You can trust the coat and size, and often the personality, of a dog who has outgrown puppy-hood. An older or more

If you do not have the time or desire to train a puppy, an older dog may be the right choice for you.

mature dog may be housebroken and have some degree of basic house manners. Puppies are great fun, but they are work, and you can bypass that struggle with a dog who has outgrown the aggravations of adolescence.

The Puppy

If you prefer a puppy, you should first read a good book on puppy rearing before starting your search. Most puppy books include some simple exercises for puppy testing so you can discover the personality under all that fuzzy fur. The rest of the book should be a valuable resource and daily reference in dealing with a puppy's first 6 to 12 months.

Socialized Puppies

Whether pups are shelter-raised from birth or reared with foster parents, socialization with people and a varied environment is

In order to become socialized, puppies should meet as many different people and animals as possible in the first few weeks of life.

critical between 6 and 16 weeks of age. A pup who is housed alone during that period will have difficulty adjusting to the outside world. A puppy must be taken out of his kennel frequently to experience new environments or kennel shyness will result. He must spend time alone with humans at least 15 minutes every day, or he'll be socially impaired. Such a puppy will have difficulty adjusting to people and may remain suspicious or frightened of anything new or different or be highly excitable when exposed to unfamiliar things. The hyper dog, one who "freaks out," trembles in fear, and urinates, is often a product of zero to poor socialization. Make proper or at least adequate socialization a primary consideration in your puppy selection process.

A Healthy Pup

Health is of course a major concern when adopting a dog of any age. Puppies especially are vulnerable to all forms of canine disease throughout their first 16 to 20 weeks. Even puppies who have been vaccinated can contract a disease if the natural immunities from their mother overrode the vaccine. Stray dogs admitted to the shelter often bring in parasites or viruses, many of which are airborne and can easily infect a pup. Your shelter puppy should be wormed, checked for fleas and other external parasites, and

Make sure you take your adopted dog to the veterinarian as soon as you acquire him in order to get a clean bill of health.

Do your homework and find out as much as you can about the purebred dog you are considering before you take him home.

been vaccinated every two to three weeks. Adult dogs should also have received the same preventive health care as a pup. Dogs of all ages should be checked for heartworm before they are adopted.

Puppy Selection

Be sure to enlist the help of shelter personnel if you decide to adopt a puppy. Personalities emerge at a very early age, and the staff can help you select a well-balanced pup who is neither too dominant nor too insecure. They can also offer experienced opinions on the breed mix and potential size, although that's no guarantee.

Purebred vs. Mixed Breed

If you're hoping to adopt the "perfect" dog (and none will be, but yours will love you so much you'll think he is), do your research first. Learn all you can about the breeds or breed combinations you're considering. Ask your veterinarian or a friend's veterinarian what breed(s) he or she would recommend for your family and lifestyle. The source of your adopted dog, whether breeder, breed rescue, or a shelter, should be able to explain breed differences and help match you with a suitable companion. There are also excellent books on canine personality and pet selection—read them.

Enlist the help of shelter personnel before choosing a dog. They can help you find a pet that compliments your personality.

Take in a dog show and talk to the owners of breeds that interest you. If you're considering a mixed-breed pup or adult, knowledge about different breed characteristics will make it easier to select a dog, since many will carry obvious and predictable qualities from their ancestors. If the mother of a litter is a purebred, you'll have at least half an idea about what the pups will look and perhaps act like.

While a purebred dog is more predictable in appearance and personality, the overbreeding of many popular breeds has led to health problems in many of those purebreds. Mixed-breed dogs may be healthier because nature has provided for their very survival over generations. This process of natural selection is called hybrid vigor, which is a heartiness attributed to cross-breeding in canines. Mixed breeds simply aren't as prone to hip dysplasia, heart and eye problems, or other inherited diseases that afflict purebred dogs. Purebred or mixed breed, whatever your choice, do your homework. Unfortunately many people research their automobiles far more than they do their dogs, even though the animal will live in the house and be with them for many more years than their vehicle.

Research your potential dog source as well as your dog. Ask your veterinarian, friends, and neighbors which animal shelters they would recommend. If you're considering a purebred dog, those shelters that work closely with breed rescue groups or individuals will gladly refer you to your breed person of choice.

5

The Adoption Process

· ·

You've determined you'll be a good owner, you've found the right shelter, and now you're ready to get started. First resolve to make several visits to several shelters as insurance for your adoption screening process. Your veterinarian should be able to refer you to at least one reliable shelter. The best source for a novice dog owner is a well-established shelter operated by experienced and knowledgeable people. Size isn't as important as the manner in which the shelter is managed. Large or small, it should look "maintained" and as clean as any multiple-dog confinement facility can look, considering the habits of dogs. The dogs should appear well cared for and the staff should be caring and concerned about the animals housed there.

Shelters usually operate with limited funds and may rely on volunteer help to supplement their very existence. Thus some are better than others—more efficient, knowledgeable and more particular in their care for the animals as well as for the people who might adopt them.

Shelter Policies

The actual adoption process will vary according to the policies of

each shelter or rescue organization. Both agencies will ask about your history with previous dogs, if you have a house or an apartment, and whether the dog will be left alone all day, plus other personal and canine information. That's good—the more they ask, the more they care.

A good shelter or humane society will ask you many questions in order to determine what type of home the dog will have and your commitment to caring for him.

You will fill out questionnaires, sometimes during your initial inquiry, and/or again when you receive the dog. Typical forms ask for specifics about your circumstances and living situation. Do you have children and their ages, a fenced yard, do you own or rent? Where will your pet be housed, both day and night? How do you plan to care for the dog—exercise, housetraining, training, grooming, health care? What's your dog history; have you owned a dog before and what happened? (If previous dogs were hit by cars or some other careless tragedy befell them, especially at an early age, shelters will seriously question and explore those circumstances before they release a dog.) If the client is adamant and refuses the educational efforts of the staff, he may be denied an animal.

If you own or have owned other dogs, you'll need to provide veterinary references. Responsible shelters always follow up and call the named veterinarian to verify the animals have had proper health care. They often discover the vet never saw the dog in question.

Some shelters require written permission from a landlord if you live in a rental unit. Many shelters and almost all rescues want to meet all members of the family before approving an adoption. The more detailed the screening process, the better chance that the dog's rehoming will be permanent and successful. The last thing shelters and rescues want is a dog that bounces from one home to another, subjected to all the stress involved with every relocation.

Some shelters provide a complete battery of shots before releasing a dog; others may give only a parvo and rabies shot and require the family to follow up with a more complete health exam and vaccinations. Each agency operates according to the funds available, which can seriously limit the health care of their canine charges.

Since most rescue dogs live in foster care with other dogs, they are usually fully vaccinated before being adopted. Rescue adoption fees can vary—most organizations and shelters agree that if you can't afford the adoption fee, you can't afford to own a dog.

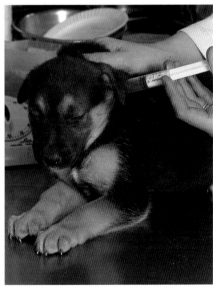

Some shelters will provide vaccinations for your dog in order to start him on the road to good health.

Spay/Neuter

If the dog you choose is still intact, you can expect a spay/neuter agreement as a pre-condition to the adoption. Many shelters

Pets for Seniors

Many shelters waive the typical adoption fees for senior citizens as a community service. Occasionally, area veterinarians also offer special pet care rates to seniors. These contributions are due to the many studies that have proven that pets are a potent anti-aging tonic for the elderly. Seniors who own dogs are more active, have lower blood pressure, make fewer trips to the doctor, suffer less depression, and make friends more easily. Pets also provide seniors with a sense of security. Studies also have shown that seniors take better care of their pets and better care of themselves. (Of course, these are all the same great reasons why people of any age should own a dog.)

won't relinquish a dog until after it is altered. Others offer a special rate for the surgery, and you may be required to show proof after the dog has been altered.

Rescue groups always insist on spaying/neutering, and for good reason. Most of the dogs they care for are the result of irresponsible breedings, and their fate could have been averted had the sire and dam been unable to reproduce. Most groups alter their dogs before placing them, rather than risk a new owner's failure to do so. A few require follow-up proof of alteration and will not hesitate to reclaim a dog if the family doesn't follow through.

The spay/neuter process is good for the dog as well as the dog population. Females spayed before their first heat cycle will never suffer from uterine or ovarian cancer, a common killer of unspayed bitches, nor will they contract pyometra, a life-threatening disease of the uterus that occurs most frequently in females over six years of age. Your female will be cleaner without the mess of estrus fluids, and you won't have amorous males lurking about your yard.

In males, neutering not only prevents testicular and other male cancers, it also eliminates the urge to roam in search of romance and reduces aggresive tendencies toward other male dogs.

Contrary to popular belief, spaying/neutering does not make a dog fat. Only too much food or too little exercise produces chubby dogs. Spaying/neutering is the best gift you can give your dog—and the dog world.

Spaying or neutering will help control the pet population and protect your dog from certain diseases of the reproductive organs.

Evaluating the Shelter Dog

Once you've completed the research and shelter forms, you can begin the real work of finding your dog. Whether your choice is purebred or mixed breed, you should discuss your preferences with shelter personnel. Ask questions about different canine characteristics and behaviors. Which of their dogs are owner turn-ins and which ones came in as strays or through animal control? Dogs relinquished by their owners often arrive with their history, which may or may not have been embellished by a well-meaning owner who hopes "good references" will aid in the animal's adoption.

Most strays have questionable backgrounds, but responsible shelters use the state-mandated three- to seven-day holding period to evaluate a dog's temperament for soundness and adoption potential. Animals with serious health or behavior problems are, out of necessity, euthanized. Shelters don't want any dog to be reshuffled, and they do their best to place the adoptable ones in good, permanent homes. Their evaluation isn't necessarily a guarantee of a dog's disposition, but it's a good beginning.

If the shelter or rescue person doesn't volunteer a particular dog's history or enough information, ask. Is this dog good with kids or other dogs, or cats if you happen to own one? If your children are grown, but your grandkids or neighbor's kids visit, you need to make sure this is a child-friendly animal. Does the dog appear to be housetrained? Is there a particular reasons why the dog behaves as he does—jumps constantly, cringes at an outstretched hand, urinates when petted? The more advance information you gather, the better prepared you'll be to select the right dog for you and your family.

Getting Acquainted with a Dog

Armed with the shelter's references and observations, it's time for you to evaluate the dogs who seem to fit your future dog's profile. Browse the kennels of each facility and carefully observe the dogs. Some shelters have history and/or information cards attached to each kennel or run, such as "Good with children," "housetrained," "some obedience training." Many facilities have get-acquainted rooms where you can spend time with individual dogs, away from the din and incessant barking that fill the kennel areas.

The best bets for adoption are dogs who appear stable and comfortable despite the chaotic kennel atmosphere. While it's true that shelter dogs may exhibit some unusual behaviors because they have been uprooted and are reacting to a stressful kennel environment, a dog who appears shy or cowers in the corner of his space may in reality be a shy or fearful dog and be

Most shelters will let you play with and handle the dog you are interested in. A dog's body language conveys a lot about how he is feeling.

difficult to rehabilitate. Avoid any dog who growls, bares his teeth, or shows signs of overt aggression toward visitors at his space. The dog may have been abused, be aggressive by nature, or simply be having a bad day, but whatever the reason, he is not a candidate for successful rehoming. Be sure to mention signs of aggression to the shelter staff in case they're unaware of the behavior.

While touring the kennel areas, talk calmly and quietly to the dogs and observe their reaction to your overtures. Look for happy wagging tails; not all wagging postures are friendly signals. How does the dog respond to a calm and friendly outstretched hand? Does the dog stare or raise the hackles on his back? These can be signs of dominance or suspicion and shouldn't be ignored.

The dog you select should allow you to pet him gently and should not be overly fearful or aggressive.

Avoid dogs who appear overly fearful or ones who display signs of submissive urination. Fearful and submissive behaviors may or may not be cured. Also look at the dog's hygiene habits in his run. A dog who eliminates all over his space then walks through his stools might be difficult to housetrain.

Concentrate only on those dogs who appear friendly and stable. A questionable dog may be worth saving, but are you willing and able to take on that task? Can you subject your family to the problems and the risks involved?

Promise yourself you won't fall in love or make your selection with your heart, unless the dog who steals it is a good candidate for rehoming. Be willing to wait and look again…and again. Try not to feel guilty and take a dog just to save him, as difficult as that may be. The dog must be right for you or he'll end up back at the shelter.

Health Considerations

While this issue may seem obvious, you should look also for a healthy animal. When evaluating potential adoptees at a shelter or rescue source, be sure the animal appears robust and healthy. Any discharge or foul odor from the dog's eyes, nose, or ears, any open sores or scabby areas, or a lack of energy or lethargic manner, are indicators of poor health. A dull dry coat, bloated rib cage, or constant scratching may be a sign of fleas, other internal parasites, or allergies. You should discount any animal who appears ill or has suspicious symptoms and bring those conditions to the attention of shelter personnel.

Final Decision

Once you've narrowed your choices to one or more dogs, ask a shelter worker to accompany you and the dog into the designated visiting area if they offer one. Again, observe the dog and his

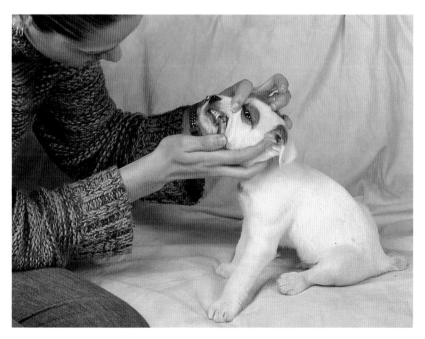

Make sure the dog you choose is healthy looking and curious about you and his surroundings.

comfort level with the shelter staff. How does the dog respond to the shelter person and does he act differently toward you and your family? Often a dog with a dominant personality is polite and well-behaved with authoritative, experienced humans, but will resist control by anyone he senses to be unsure or subordinate. While these are not insurmountable problems, you have to recognize them and be prepared to deal with a dog who might try to take over your house and constantly challenge you for "Top Dog" status.

While visiting with each dog under consideration, interact with the dog through play activities. Roll a ball to fetch or toss a squeaky toy. Is the dog happy and playful with you? Does he welcome playful petting and handling? When petted does he shrink away? That's not too bad as long as the dog warms up to you after a few minutes of gentle overtures. Test the dog's

Interacting with a dog in the shelter through play and activity will allow you to observe his behavior and temperament.

response, if any, to "Sit" and "Down" obedience commands. Use food treats as rewards to see if the dog will comply with your requests.

Walk around the room and chat lightly with the dog. Does he follow you, cower, or run away? A very nervous dog who shies away may be difficult to rehabilitate. Will he walk willingly on a leash? If space prevents you from evaluating the dog in this manner, you might visit another time or try a different facility.

Certain behaviors should send up a warning flag. You should be aware of them up front and be prepared to deal with them or look for a different animal. Your adopted dog will be with you for many years; these are just security measures to help to ensure a happy life together.

Adopting from Breed Rescue

If you adopt your dog from a breed rescue group, most of the suggested evaluation may have been handled by a foster family. Responsible rescue groups generally place their dogs in foster care for a period of time to evaluate the dog, his temperament, and any prior training to determine the best future environment for the dog. A rescue representative interviews prospective adopters in person and with written questionnaires to determine the family's needs and if they would provide a proper loving home for one of their breed. Rescues are usually more stringent in their adoption criteria (fenced yards, family circumstances, etc.), while shelters seldom have the luxury of such selective placement. Rescues sometimes offer a trial period to see if the dog and new family will be compatible. If you decide to adopt through a breed rescue, you should still research the breed to make sure it's right for you. The more knowledgeable you are, the better your chances that the rescue committee will approve you as an adopter and pair you with the right dog.

Most dogs in breed rescue have been evaluated by a foster family. These people have lived with the dog and can tell you a lot about his personality.

If you haven't already asked all the important questions, be sure to do so before you sign the final paperwork and take your new dog home. You've made a grand decision and you can look forward to many years of loving companionship, especially if you did your pre-adoption homework. The only heartache in adoption is that you can't save them all.

6

Preparing for Homecoming

. . . .

Dog Supplies

Make shopping for your new dog a grand adventure. This will be your dog's personal wardrobe. Envision your new dog as you select each item on your list and how much he'll enjoy having his own "stuff." Tailor your purchases to suit your new dog—small sizes for little guys, etc. Most good-quality dog supplies are available in pet stores.

Food Dishes or Bowls

You'll need two non-tippable, stainless steel or heavy stoneware bowls, one each for food and water. Remember how often you'll have to pick it up when you look at a heavy stoneware bowl that matches your decor. Non-breakable is practical, but plastic is too easily chewed and doesn't sanitize well. An older dog may need raised bowls so less pressure is put on its joints. These are readily available.

Leashes

A 4- to 6-foot nylon leash is fine for a young pup, but an older dog will need a 6-foot leather or strong cloth lead, especially in obedience class. A "flexi-lead," an 8- to 20-foot retractable leash

Have all your dog supplies ready for your new canine family member before he gets home.

that reels in automatically, is especially handy for exercise in public places.

Collars

Nylon or leather buckle or safety-snap collars work best for most dogs. Rolled leather is often preferred for long-haired breeds, although some leather dyes may stain the fur. Chain or "choke" collars are for specific training purposes only and should never be left on the dog at any other time. A halter is useful for taking a dog who pulls on a walk—it hurts less and causes less damage.

Identification Tags

Proper identification is a must! Avoid ID tags with an "S" hook attachment; they snag carpeting and bedding and easily fall off; key or "O" ring attachments are more secure. Many sporting dog owners prefer a brass plate ID that is riveted on the collar. Never include the dog's name on his tag; it will allow a thief to call your dog. Some owners include an extra line on the ID tag or plate as an additional precaution: "Dog needs medication," or "Reward" in hopes of encouraging a lost or stolen dog's swift return.

Tattoos and Microchips

At the earliest time possible, your new dog should also be permanently identified with a tattoo or microchip. Many owners opt for both. Stories abound about dogs who have been returned to their owners because of

The right leash will make long walks with your dog more enjoyable.

such identification. The best example lies with the new AKC Companion Animal Recovery program, with over 1,677,120 enrolled animals in 2003. Also, as of 2003, 126,034 lost pets have been successfully reunited with their owners. Some shelters offer microchip services, as to most veterinarians.

Grooming Tools

You'll need a brush, comb, nail clippers and shampoo, all selected according to your dog's breed(s) or coat type. A wire brush and comb are suitable for long-haired dogs; a bristle brush for shorter coats. A slicker brush also works well on most coats. Your veterinarian, groomer, or shelter personnel can help you choose the proper equipment for your individual dog.

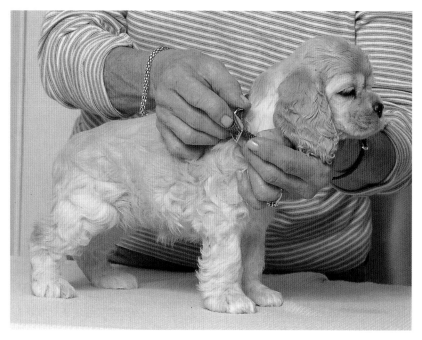

If your dog is lost, a collar with an identification tag can aid in his safe return.

Ask your veterinarian to demonstrate the nail clippers during your first visit. Nails should be clipped regularly, or you'll have snags and scratches in your house and on yourself. Some dogs object to having their feet handled or nails trimmed. If a large dog resists and a struggle ensues, the dog can become distrustful of other handling as well. Pay close attention to how your veterinarian handles the dog during nail trimming. If your dog objects, use treats to form a pleasant association—you may have to settle for one foot at a time.

Toys

These should also be selected specifically for your new special dog. All dogs need chew toys, just make sure they're safe. You can trust Nylabone® chews, rope toys such as Nylafloss® (for chewing only, not for tugging!), hard rubber balls or Rhinos (stuff them with a small dab of peanut butter or cheese to keep your dog amused for hours). Most dogs enjoy rawhide chews, but they should be used with supervision to prevent the dog from swallowing too large a chunk and choking. Too many rawhide treats can also cause loose stools and intestinal blockage, so use them with discretion.

Be careful of small toys or balls that could be swallowed and squeaky toys with eyes or parts that can be chewed off. Wooly stuffed toys are fun, but beware—some dogs shred instead of cuddle.

A safe chew toy can keep your dog's teeth healthy and keep him occupied and out of trouble.

When offering all these goodies to your dog, limit his choices to three or four toys at a time. Like children, dogs can become bored with too many toys at once. Rotating his toys will keep his interest peaked.

Dog Beds

Your dog will need a sturdy bed of his own, and there are many to choose from. Lambswool pads, cushiony cedar bags, and wicker baskets are comfy and attractive, but some dogs chew them up to relieve their stress or boredom. Fiberglass beds lined with blankets are not very tasty and are fairly indestructible. Initially, the dog may shred the bedding material, so it's practical to use an old blanket or heavy towel to line a bed or crate.

A crate is a very important tool for housetraining your dog, as well as keeping him safe when you cannot supervise him.

Crate

Don't cringe at the idea of a crate; it will be the best friend your dog has besides yourself. You'll need a dog crate that will accommodate your dog's adult size. The Nylabone® Fold Away Pet Carrier collapses and folds for easy storage when it is not in use. You will learn about crate training and housetraining later in this book.

Dogproofing Your House

Once you have your dog supplies laid in, it's time to examine your house and property. Do a room-by-room house check to make sure your home is safe for your new dog (and vice-versa). This is especially urgent if you're bringing home a puppy. Some hazards are more dangerous and may be fatal for a pup. You also want to eliminate anything that might create problems or temptations in order to promote the most positive environment for your new dog by avoiding unnecessary or frivolous corrections.

A New Name for Your Dog

Seems obvious enough, but how do you start? Even if your dog already has a name, most shelters suggest you rename him to remove any association with his past, especially if he's been abused. Of course pick out a name you like, but it's best to make it short and pleasant-sounding. Also, avoid using his name during corrections. Make sure your dog will be able to differentiate between his own name and your spouse and children, as well as from commands like "No," "Sit," and "Come." Then use his name with meals and other good-dog situations—he'll figure it out.

■ Fasten all electrical cords to baseboards or move them out of reach. Electrical burns can range from serious to fatal.

■ Keep all medications, cleaning agents, and similar materials out of open areas and locked up where your dog can't reach them. A curious dog or determined puppy can chew the lid off even a heavy bottle of toxic cleanser.

■ Never use pesticides, roach and rodent sprays, or poisons in any area accessible to your dog. Don't assume the dog

Baby gates can be used to keep your new dog in a safe area until he becomes trained and trustworthy in all parts of your home.

Be sure to dog proof your yard and provide him with adequate shelter as well as room to play.

won't find it—he'll surprise you by doing what you least expect.

- Always keep the lid down on the toilet and avoid the use of bowl cleaners in case your dog gets into the water despite your best efforts. It seems all dogs are born with a radar that attracts them to a toilet bowl.

- Never throw chicken or turkey bones in your garbage container, and keep the trash secured where your dog can't dig after other tempting garbage that could choke or harm him.

- Antifreeze will kill your dog. Animals are attracted to its sweet taste, and even a few drops can kill an average-size dog. Clean up all spills immediately and keep containers locked or well secured.

■ Check your house and yard for plants that might be toxic to your dog and place all house plants out of a puppy's reach. You can obtain a list of dangerous plants from your veterinarian or local library. Some common house and yard plants can make your dog extremely ill or can be fatal if ingested.

■ Weed killers and other herbicides are toxic to your dog as well as to children. Some have residual effects for up to several days. Read the bag carefully. If you use a lawn service, have a serious discussion with your yard man. Many dog owners prefer to live with a few weeds rather than risk their dog's long-term health.

■ Remove cigarettes and cigarette butts from ashtrays and other dog-convenient places. Ingested cigarettes can lead to nicotine poisoning.

■ At Christmas, keep all decorations out of your dog's reach. Puppies especially can dispose of a dangling ornament in the blink of an eye. Chocolate is also highly toxic to dogs, as it contains a chemical called theobromine they are unable to metabolize. A 12-ounce bag of chocolate chips can kill a small dog; two bags would put a larger dog at serious risk. The danger is proportionate to the dog's weight, so hide those chocolate Santas and other treats.

■ Consult your veterinarian before using any flea control products, especially on puppies under 16 weeks of age. Many are toxic to young dogs, and combining certain products can cause a toxic, even fatal, reaction in dogs of any age.

■ Conduct a thorough check of your fencing or dog run/kennel to be sure there are no holes or weak areas your new dog could slip through.

■ Check all windows and screens for any that are loose and would allow a dog or puppy to fall through. Every year, the Humane Society of the United States reports that dogs, cats, and puppies fall out of windows that were unsecured (or unsupervised!) and were injured or killed.

Everything you do to dogproof your home will not only make it safer for your dog, but will eliminate the possibility of "No-No's" or situations where you must correct the dog. The more positive the environment, the more successfully your dog will become a well-behaved member of your family.

Dogproof the Kids

Did you know you need to dogproof your children at the same time you dogproof your house? Teach your children and their friends that this dog or puppy is a living creature who is a friend and companion, not a toy to sit on or drag about. Show them how to be gentle and properly handle the dog. Never leave young children alone with puppy or adult dog; a playful nip is painful and can easily break the skin, leaving the child fearful and resentful of the animal. Conversely, even innocent child's play can result in serious injury to a puppy or small dog.

It's very important that you teach your child the proper way to approach and interact with a dog. "Jed," owned by Eric Nathanson, and Alice are getting to know each other.

Teach older children the correct way to hold a

Extra Caution With Infants and Toddlers

If your child is under three years old, you should think twice about getting a dog, especially a puppy. Kids and dogs might be twice the fun, but they are also double the work. It's great for kids to grow up with a dog, but kids under three years of age don't understand animals. Both require your full-time attention, and when it comes to prioritizing, the dog will always come in second. And because neither dog nor child yet understands dog or kid rules, almost everything will be a "No-No," which creates a negative environment for both of them. It's best to wait until the child is older and able to follow instructions about living with a dog. Many breeders won't even sell a pup to families with children under five years old; it's in their dog's best interest.

Meanwhile, expose your youngsters to sweet-tempered dogs who love being with friends or other family members, or perhaps offer to dog-sit occasionally so your child will gradually learn how to treat an animal until such time when they can have a dog for their own best friend.

puppy or small dog, with a firm grip under the chest and stomach so the pup can't wiggle and fall. Never allow them to carry the dog around; he can easily injure himself in even a short fall.

Teach your children to respect a dog's needs and privacy. They must allow him time and space for naps and meals and time-out. Emphasize that puppies and dogs need down time just like children do. Instruct them not to take the dog's food or disturb him when he's eating or sleeping; that's how dog bites happen.

Explain to your children that these rules apply to all dogs, not just your own. Tell them that all dogs are not friendly like theirs, and that some may bite. Teach them never to approach a strange dog and to always ask permission from the owner before they pet a dog. Show them how to approach a dog to pet it,

Communication and consistency are the keys to helping your adopted dog adjust to his new home.

from the front with an outstretched hand for the dog to sniff first. Urge them to avoid any dog who growls or snarls or runs away.

Don't expect your children to be the primary caretakers of your dog. Sure they need to learn responsibility, but the dog's welfare is too important to be placed in the hands of kids who will be just that—kids. Let your child share in the caring for the dog, but an adult member of the household should be fully responsible for the animal.

Thinking Like a Dog

Before you collect your dog to begin his new life in your home, you should have a good understanding of canine behavior and the canine thinking process. Of course, you know dogs don't rationalize in human terms, but you need to understand how your dog thinks if you're going to communicate successfully with him and teach him the rules of his new home.

You want a good friend, one you can be proud of, one who'll walk tall beside you. To reach that end, you have to master Canine Communication 101. Dogs are very social creatures; they are pack animals who, thanks to their wolf ancestors, instinctively sense and respond to a pecking order to establish the boundaries in their world. If a dog doesn't know who's in charge, he feels insecure and, unconsciously but instinctively, will always be inching up the ladder to be the boss, the one in charge, because if no one leads, he'll have to assume that position himself.

Life in the Pack

In the wild, in the pack, everything in a canid's life comes after the leader, the alpha dog, is satisfied, has had his fill, or gives permission. Dogs are not unhappy with this arrangement. Rather,

Taking on the role of leader in your relationship with your dog will help him to feel more confident and secure.

they feel secure knowing they have a leader who is strong, protects and guards the pack, and keeps other pack members in their proper place. So social is their nature they are happy knowing they have pleased their leader; so it is with you and your new dog as well.

How do you achieve this status as your dog's new pack leader? Communicate through obedience and housetraining with a firm but loving hand. That process will make him feel safe and confident in his new home. (Specific training techniques are discussed later in this book.)

Positive and Negative Reinforcements

All dogs are learning machines. Some breeds are better students because of their ancestry, but every dog will try to please his leader if the dog is treated with respect and understands what is expected of him. Today's obedience instructors find it's better to train a dog with positive reinforcement instead of the older methods that required hitting, pushing, jerking, and other forms of punishment.

Dogs learn best through repetition and reward. Using positive reinforcement, lots of "Good dog!" praise, and occasional bits of a food treat, good behavior is rewarded, the dog feels good, and so repeats that behavior. It's also true that if the dog does something naughty that he feels is fun or makes him feel good (as in sleeping on the sofa or stealing food) and gets away with it, even once, he will surely do it again. (Your lesson here is never take your eyes off the dog until he is completely trustworthy.)

Be Consistent

Consistency is the key to success with any method of training. By applying the same word to each desired behavior when it occurs, the dog will soon repeat the action when he hears the command word. This principle applies to puppies as well as adult dogs. By

Always remain composed when training or disciplining your adopted dog, and remember that praise and encouragement are great training motivators.

using food or other lures, you can initiate some actions, such as sit and down, and learning will automatically follow. With other behaviors, such as housetraining, you must wait until the dog performs outside (as he surely will!) and immediately apply the praise.

The Here and Now

Dogs learn in the present tense. Even seconds later is too late. You can use a correction only if you catch the dog at the exact moment of a naughty deed, such as eliminating on your carpet. Only then will he understand a strong voice correction, such as "No!" as you whisk him out the door to where he should be going. Corrections that come after the act, whatever that act may be, even when a dog knows better, is always too late.

An Ounce of Prevention

Preventing mischief before it happens is better than correcting it, especially if your dog learns a lesson in the process. For example, your dog lingers at the kitchen counter, eyeing the slab of beef you've set out for tonight's dinner—you know what he's thinking about! A stern "No!" will change his mind before the deed is done. Just watch him lower his posture and slip away. You've averted a disaster, and your dog thinks you're a mind reader.

No Hitting Allowed

Never, ever hit your dog with your hand or swat him with a newspaper or other object. That will not teach him a thing and will only make him hand-shy and afraid of you. (Please don't confuse fear with respect.) You should also remember that dogs do not understand human anger and will only become confused and frightened when you are angry.

Your dog's ancestors were probably bred to perform certain functions. Your dog will be happiest if given a job to do that utilizes these natural abilities.

You often hear it said that that dog knew he was naughty because he had a "guilty look" when his owner came home and found the wastebasket upturned and spilled. In reality, the dog was reacting to his owner's behavior and connecting that anger with the mess on the floor, not the fact that he put it there two hours ago. What's obvious to us often is not clear to the dog.

Working for a Living

Once the dog has mastered certain commands, you can use them to reinforce his behavior. These obedience commands are valuable disciplinary tools and should be used as reminders that you're the one in charge. If your dog jumps up, give a "Sit" command and insist that he sits until released from that position. Be sure to praise him while he's sitting and tell him what a good fellow he is. Make him sit before he gets his food dish, before he goes out the door, and as soon as he comes in. Make him "Down-Stay" while you read the paper. Scratch his head for being good, but make him stay and praise him when he listens.

Never engage in rough-housing games with an untrained dog. Power-struggle play activities that invite your dog to challenge your "Top Dog" status encourage canine aggression, and the last thing you need is an aggressive dog who thinks he's the boss.

Play obedience games instead. Your dog will think you're a fun pal and learn to enjoy obedience in the process. Once he understands "Sit" and "Down," give him unexpected commands in a happy voice, a super-quick food reward, a big hug and silly talk. Run the commands together: "Sit," "Down," "Sit," "Down," then a huge "Free!" with hugs and kisses. Act as silly as a puppy; your dog won't tell a soul.

7

Welcome Home

· ·

A t last, the day has come to bring your new friend home. It's
an exciting time, but you should keep in mind some
important considerations.

The Transition

Make every effort to pick up your dog over a long weekend, on
vacation days, or another period when you'll have two or more
days to spend with him. That will help minimize the risk of
separation anxiety when you do leave him alone. It goes without
saying that you should never bring a dog home at Christmas or at
other hectic holidays.

At the shelter or rescue home, allow time to learn every shred of
information about your dog's background, if you haven't already
done so. Review health matters and get the paperwork on his
vaccinations. Find out what kind of food he's eating. If you plan
to feed something else, it's wise to mix the two foods together
and gradually increase the amount of new ration to prevent
intestinal upset from a new dog food.

Bring your new collar, leash, and ID tags; don't rely on whatever the dog might have. The leash is vital, since the dog may object to going with you. Bring a companion or other family member to help collect the dog. He may be afraid of cars or resist entering your vehicle, and you'll need a helper to comfort him during the trip home. Changing environments is very stressful for a dog, and fewer distractions will minimize the stress.

Patience and Understanding

When you're stocking up your dog essentials, be sure to lay in a generous supply of patience and understanding—you'll probably need both during your dog's first weeks at home. Of course, you plan to love this dog forever, but he doesn't know that yet. He may act frightened or shy; in fact, he probably will. He might misbehave or try to run away. He's naturally insecure about his new surroundings.

Make your dog's homecoming as peaceful and uneventful as possible to allow him time to adjust and get comfortable.

A Peaceful Home

Make the dog's home-coming as peaceful and uneventful as possible. Forget any welcome home celebrations with relatives or your children's friends. Children, especially, should not smother the dog with too much attention and excitement. This may be his second or third home, so he needs quiet time to adjust to his new space and learn to trust his new human family.

Walk the dog on a leash around your yard and

through allowable areas of the house so he can sniff and investigate every nook and corner. Show him his water supply and eating area if it's separate from his water bowl. Don't assume the dog will automatically know his dog things. Introduce him to his crate and/or sleeping area. The crate should be kept in a quiet place, but not removed from activity so the dog won't feel isolated from the family.

Learning the Ropes

For the first day or two, set your cooking timer for 60 minutes and, every hour, take your dog to the same place in the yard where he can relieve himself. Even if he's housetrained, the stress of a new environment could set his habits back. Your passwords are still praise, patience and persistence. Puppies, of course, require the entire gamut of training procedures, since they have no history to draw on. Read that book you bought on puppy training. Check out another book or two on obedience training if your new dog is an adult or older puppy. (For some book suggestions, see the Resources section.)

Although your adopted dog will prefer to spend most of his time bonding with you, provide him with many opportunities to socialize with other dogs and people. This will help him to become a well-behaved and well-adjusted canine citizen.

These first days are important in establishing your role as your dog's pack leader. He needs to learn that you're in charge, or he'll gladly assume that chore himself. He also needs to feel wanted and loved. That means quality time, constant supervision, and playtime, and confinement when you can't be with him. No free time for a while; he doesn't know the rules and could easily misbehave because he doesn't know better.

He also needs to be socialized like any other new member of the family. Do this at home for the first week or so, then out and about so he can become confident in his new world. In the house, keep him with you while you read or watch TV. Have him tag along during your normal household routine of cooking, laundry, and other chores to maximize your time together. It's important to just be there.

Gradually expand your daily walks to include new places, sounds and smells—the neighborhood park, grocery store, other shops, a friend's backyard. Each new adventure will intrigue and stimulate him.

Your children's new-dog rules should apply to everyone. Don't lavish heaps of attention on the dog and don't cave in if he's being demanding. Maintain a calm and quiet atmosphere until the dog settles into a comfortable routine.

Routine is important to his adjustment. Your daily activities should be fairly consistent so the dog learns he can depend on you. A newly adopted dog is often very insecure in a new environment – can you blame him? He's been abandoned once, maybe more. It's your job to build his confidence and convince him that he—and you—are here to stay.

Practice these leadership exercises as the situations occur throughout the day. They will help turn your puppy into a confident, friendly dog that is eager to please all members of the family – adults and children alike.

- Have your dog sit and wait while you go through outside doors first.

- Have your dog wait for her meal until after people have had their dinner.

- Teach your dog to accept being touched while he eats.

- Gently move your dog out of the way if she is lying in your path.

- Have your dog obey a request like "sit" before receiving attention.

- Pet your dog with long, slow strokes starting at the top of head and continuing to the shoulders.

- Play games like fetch, with you in control of the toys at the end.

- Teach your dog that hands are not appropriate chew toys.

- Practice touching and handling your dog's feet, mouth, and ears.

- Speak in a soft, high-pitched, praising voice so your dog is eager to pay attention.

Other Pets

If you have another family dog you must plan carefully for the introduction. Never bring a rescue or shelter dog into your home and let the two dogs introduce themselves. Your normally sweet dog may resent this new intruder and will have at it before you can catch your breath.

It's best to introduce the dogs on neutral ground, at a nearby park or isolated public area. Both dogs should be on leash, with one

Under your supervision, introduce your dog to other pets carefully and let them become friends on their own terms.

person to attend each dog. Be sure to maintain a loose leash, as tension on the leash may signal to each dog that the other is a threat and he could assume an aggressive posture. Allow both dogs to approach each other and sniff for about 10 to 15 seconds. Use verbal praise and happy talk when they show signs of normal curiosity. Then call them apart in a casual manner without pulling on the leash. If there were no signs of aggression, repeat the meeting for slightly longer. If the dogs play bow and wag their tails, let them play together with leashes on for security, then take them for a walk together, both on lead. Repeat the on-leash play process in your backyard. Supervise the dogs' time together until a firm friendship is established; some take more time to bond than others. Feed them separately but at the same time (very often the subordinate dog will choose not to eat his food until the dominant dog is finished with his meal) and don't allow them to share toys until they prove reliable together. Be fair and equal with your attention so your original dog doesn't feel neglected or left out.

Both dogs will have to establish a pecking order between them, and some minor scuffling may ensue. Do not allow or at least minimize the opportunities for disputes to arise, and never allow them to escalate. Separate the animals calmly and without punishment. It's always better to deflect a fight with distractions or obedience commands. If serious or prolonged fighting occurs, contact your shelter or adoption coordinator for further advice.

If you have a cat, don't force an introduction and don't restrain the cat. Just make sure it has an escape route when you bring your new dog home. They will usually work things out on their own terms.

Crate Training

The use of a crate is the best way to allow your dog to get away from it all and have his own space. It's also great for housetraining as well as dogproofing. The crate is a critical key to the success of your new dog's adoption program. You and other family members or friends may view the crate as cruel or inhumane, but your dog doesn't see it that way.

From the dog's perspective, he now has a room of his own, a place where he feels safe and secure, a sanctuary, an indoor doghouse if you will. A crate satisfies the natural "den" instinct that he inherited from his ancestors. From his perspective, it's not a cage he can't get out of—it's his very own territory where humans can't get in! You can appreciate it as a place where he can't get into trouble, rather than left to his other instincts that lead to shredding and chewing whatever isn't nailed down.

The crate then offers peace of mind for both you and your dog. You can leave your dog home alone knowing he, as well as your

A crate will provide your dog with a quiet den in which he can retreat and relax.

home and possessions, are comfortable and protected. This also spares your dog the fear and confusion he'll endure when you come home and discover he chewed your sofa cushions or antique table legs while you were gone. Even if you don't scold, you'll still be upset and he'll sense it.

With crate training, you can confine your dog when you have guests, children, or anyone else who might overly excite him or lead him to disruptive behavior. You also can travel safely with your dog. He's tucked into his own canine baby seat and can't jump in your lap, an obvious safety precaution for both of you when you're motoring on the interstate. Your crated dog will be welcome at motels, and even your grumpy aunt can't complain if he's crated when you visit.

A crate's greatest value is in housetraining your dog or puppy. It allows you to capitalize on a canine's natural instinct not to soil his den and to establish a regular routine for outdoor elimination. The crate will also prevent accidents at night and whenever he must be left alone.

Although the crate will be your dog's favorite place to be, make sure you don't abuse it. Never place your dog in his crate in anger. Also, a crate is never recommended for a dog who must be

The crate should be a safe and secure place for your dog; never place him in his crate as punishment.

left alone for long periods of time. As a general rule, a dog shouldn't be crated for more than four hours at a time; puppies never more than three. Leave the radio on during your absence; the sound of music and a human voice will soothe him while you're gone.

If you can't tend to your dog for long periods of time, enlist the aid of a neighbor or friend who can come over to let the dog out to relieve himself and stretch his legs. If no such person is available, consider using a doggie day care on those extra-long days.

Selecting a Crate

There are many types of crates available; however, an excellent choice is the Nylabone® Fold Away Pet Carrier. This crate folds up for easy storage when you are not using it. The crate should be large enough for an adult dog to lie down without being cramped and sit up without hitting his head. This size may be

Select a crate that is big enough for your dog to sit, stand, and turn around in comfortably.

tough to predict if you have a mixed-breed pup who could grow beyond your expectations; you'll just have to take your best guess. Your vet or shelter worker should be able to suggest the proper size. It's best to have the crate set up when you bring your new dog home so you can begin crate conditioning right away.

Crate Conditioning

Although your dog will feel secure when he's crated, you still want him to feel like he's part of the family unit. Place the crate in a "people" area of the house, such as a corner of the family room or kitchen so he won't be totally isolated. It may not be the most attractive piece of furniture in the room, but it does come in handy as an extra tabletop.

At night, move the crate into your bedroom so your dog won't feel left alone again. Sleeping in his crate next to your bed will also continue the bonding process. A puppy especially needs to know you're close by even when he's snoozing. You'll also be able to hear him stir or whimper if he has to go out, which will aid in housetraining. Puppies rarely "hold it" through the night, and even adult dogs in a new and strange environment may need to relieve themselves due to stress or anxiety.

Make the crate a cozy place; toss in a couple of chew toys, such as Nylabone® chews, plus an old towel or blanket so he has something comfy to curl up on. Leave out items of value in case he shreds them and include something you can wash if he soils it. An article of clothing, like an old bathrobe or sweatshirt with your scent on it, sometimes works to comfort the dog. You may have to experiment with a crate rug or towel to see what works—every dog is different.

Allow your dog to get used to the crate by feeding him and giving him treats or toys whenever he goes inside. Soon, he will expect good things from crate training.

Teach your dog to accept his new den by tossing a bit of a food treat into the crate while he's watching. Leave the food in the crate until he takes it, then praise him when he does. Some dogs will dash right in, while others are more skeptical and have to muster up their courage to investigate. You can also feed the first few

Sleeping Partners

It's never a good idea to allow your dog to sleep with you (at least not in the beginning!). To a dog, being on your bed means equality, and it will seriously diminish your leadership position. For people who like a furry critter in their bed, wait until the dog is thoroughly trained and respects your authority. Make bed-sharing a privilege gained only by permission, and he must also learn the "Off" command. If he refuses to leave when asked, won't share his bed space, or shows even a small sign of dominance, like a curled lip or muted growl, the bed becomes off limits—the same for your children's beds.

Gradually extend the amount of time you leave your dog in the crate until he can stay happily for three to four hours.

meals in the crate with the crate door open to create a pleasant association. Leave those chew toys in the crate so he can amuse himself when he's crated and awake. Use a kennel command such as "Kennel" or "Crate" when the dog goes in. Remember that important dog rule about word association: consistency.

After he's been going in and out comfortably, gradually close the door and leave it closed for a minute or two, then release him—no big fanfare coming out, make it a non-event, and no treats or big hugs so he won't be anxious to come out for those rewards. His reward is simply being with you once again.

Don't allow him to bark while crated. Whether he's protesting confinement or just singing along with Sinatra, he must learn to be quiet in his den. Never release him from his crate when he's noisy, or he'll think barking got him out.

Even if things don't go smoothly at first, don't weaken and don't worry. You're doing your dog a favor by preventing mischief when he's left alone, so it's worth the effort. Almost every dog will accept crating; it's just a matter of time.

Once he's staying in the closed crate, extend the period of time he spends in there; it shouldn't take more than a day or two to accomplish this. Now you can move ahead to establish a solid housetraining routine.

Crates and Housetraining

In the beginning, take your dog out every hour or two until he gets used to the idea of going out. Use the same door each time, and until he's reliable, confine your dog to the area of the house nearest the door he's supposed to use. (If he's at the other end of the house and has to relieve himself, he won't know where the exit is.) Baby gates make a good containment system. Then gradually introduce him to other allowable areas of his new home, one room at a time, so all these strange surroundings won't overwhelm him. It's less stressful for a dog of any age to explore new places on a limited basis, and it won't upset the housetraining apple cart.

Take him to the same place outside every time and praise him like a hero for doing his job. Use key words, such as "Get busy" or "Hurry up," so he'll learn what these little trips outside are all about. When he goes, repeat the key word along with the praise, "Good boy, get busy, good boy, get busy." He'll soon figure it out.

Even if you have a fenced backyard, you still have to accompany your adopted dog on every bathroom outing, rain or snow, midnight or 3 am, so you can be sure he's done his business *and* so you can lay on the praise. Remember those key words – and the three "Ps"—persistence, patience, and praise.

During the housetraining process, puppies will need to be crated more than an adult dog because they have so little bladder control and they haven't learned to recognize that "gotta go" feeling in advance. A pup should be crated at night, during naps, and whenever you're not able to watch him. If your puppy falls asleep at your feet, just pick him up and place him in his crate to finish his nap. Be sure to close the door;

Many dogs are given up because of housetraining problems; however, with a regular schedule and lots of supervision, any healthy dog can be housetrained.

otherwise, guess what? He'll probably wake up, toddle out of his den to piddle, then run over to you to say hello. Behind closed doors, he'll whine or yip when he wakes up—and puppies *always* have to go when they wake up!

Take the puppy out to relieve himself every time he leaves his crate. Puppies also need to eliminate when they first wake up in the morning, after naps and playtime, within a short period after eating, and before going to bed at night.

Be observant and monitor your dog or puppy's signals when he has to go out: Sniffing the floor, starting to squat, circling at the door, maybe just walking to the door with a quick glance, then back to you are all signs that he has to eliminate. Each dog develops his own message system, and if you're not there in seconds, it will be puddle time. It's up to you to make sure he's as successful as possible to build good habits you both can live with.

When you're mopping up those messes, be sure to thoroughly disinfect and deodorize the soiled areas. His nose will know, and your dog will return to those spots if they retain his smell. Using a special odor neutralizer you can get at the pet store, saturate the spot, cover with a folded towel and place a book over the towel for 24 hours. (Then think up a clever excuse for your neighbors about why you have books all over the living room rug.)

When those little accidents happen, just bite the bullet and resolve to be more watchful. Never discipline your dog or puppy for an accident you discover after the fact. Dogs only understand this moment in time and will not connect a correction with a past

While many adopted dogs were housetrained as puppies, they may lapse in new or stressful situations or because of medical problems.

deed. Punishing him even seconds later will only create a fearful dog—you have to catch him in the act. Use a firm "No!" and whisk him outside. Praise him when he goes where you want him to. Occasionally, the shock of your sudden reprimand may even cause the dog to stop piddling and he'll finish the job outside.

Never strike a dog with your hand or a newspaper or rub his nose in his mess. Such tactics are extreme and will only cause fear and confusion in the dog and further complicate the housetraining process.

There are many books available today that specifically address issues such as housetraining and teaching house manners. Reading one or two of them will add to your arsenal of dog knowledge, make you a better and more responsible dog owner, and produce a better dog. (See Resources for recommendations.)

8

A Healthy New Life

. . . .

Regardless of your pet's health history, it is up to you to make sure that he is given the best possible health care—including regular veterinary visits, proper nutrition, ample exercise, and good grooming.

Visit the Veterinarian

Your dog's first venture into his new world should be to his veterinarian. Try to make his vet visit pleasant so he won't associate the car with a possible stressful examination in a strange environment.

First, find a vet you can trust and feel comfortable with. Friends or neighbors who have dogs are good referral sources. A good relationship with your vet will be beneficial for both of you.

Bring along the dog's health records if you have them and a stool sample on this first visit. Ask lots of questions about dog care in general: How much should he eat, how often should he be bathed, how do I trim his nails, clean his ears? Take your time, ask for demonstrations, and take notes. Also ask about heartworm medication. Your veterinarian will complete or plan the dog's

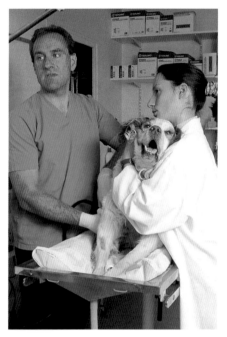

It is up to you to provide your adopted dog with the care he will need to live a long and healthy life.

vaccination schedule if needed. He also will explain that you must visit at least once a year to update your dog's shots and check for heartworm and other internal parasites.

Obtain a canine first aid guide so you can recognize emergency situations and be prepared to handle them. (Yes, they do happen in all dog families!) It's much easier—and healthier—to prevent emergency situations from happening than it is to deal with them unprepared. This is a good time to start a dog diary to keep your dog's health record current and health care information handy.

Feeding and Nutrition

Be sure to discuss dog food with your veterinarian. Most vets recommend a quality dry kibble food appropriate for each dog's age and activity level. Avoid generic and store brands as they usually are made with inferior products and will not provide complete or adequate nutrition.

Establish a meal routine and feed at the same time once or twice a day. A regular feeding schedule is especially important for your adopted dog who needs these constants in his life to feel secure again. Puppies should eat three times daily until four or five months of age, then switch to twice a day. Don't free-feed adults

Feed your adopted dog a nutritious diet that is high in fat and protein and formulated for his stage of life.

or puppies and never leave the food out for the dog to eat at his whimsy. This technique plays havoc with elimination habits and housetraining. A regular feeding schedule supports housetraining and helps prevent obesity.

Always offer the food in the same place and leave it out for about 20 minutes. If the dog doesn't eat or finish it, remove the bowl and don't add the unfinished portion to the next meal—offer the same amount each time.

Don't worry if he's off his feed his first day or two at home. Dogs are less apt to starve themselves than they are to overeat and get too fat. Never feed your dog table scraps, even if he refuses to eat his own food. If you dog is a poor eater, try a different (not cheaper) dry food or sprinkle a bit of garlic or onion powder over the food—most dogs love it! You can also try mixing a small

Your dog should have access to cool clean water at all times, especially when outside.

amount of canned food with the dry. Canned food is less nutritious and contains approximately 75 percent water, but most dogs love the flavor and will gobble their dry food if it's enhanced with a canned product.

A note of caution: No vitamins or supplements for puppies. Puppy food is especially balanced for proper growth, and adding your own goodies could affect growth patterns. Most veterinary nutritionists advise a quality puppy food only.

Allow your dog access to water at all times. For dogs of all ages, avoid heavy exercise an hour before and two hours after feeding.

Exercise

Regular exercise is as important as a good diet for your dog. Not only will it help prevent obesity (in your dog and you!), it will keep your dog physically stimulated, satisfied, and less apt to venture into seek-and-destroy missions around the house. The amount of exercise depends on the size, breed, and temperament of the dog, but as a rule, a half-hour walk twice a day will keep the average dog in decent shape. High-energy dogs might need additional activity, like fetch games. Swimming is a great all-around exercise if you have a pond nearby and a dog who thinks he's a fish (and many do!).

Agility games and exercises are also great energy expenders and fun for the owner as well as the dog. Local kennel clubs and dog training clubs may offer agility classes or access to agility equipment. Agility has grown into a major dog sport and entertainment form. Try it—you'll both love it!

Grooming and Bathing

Your dog also needs to be kept clean and groomed, according to whatever

Regular exercise is essential for your dog's physical and mental well-being.

grooming regimen your veterinarian recommends and the coat type of your dog. Use a quality dog shampoo (people shampoo is too harsh) that won't strip the natural oils from his coat.

Grooming is the hands-on part your dog will love the most. Not only will frequent (at least twice a week) brushing keep your dog handsome and presentable, it will become part of the bonding process, stroking the dog as you comb and brush, with your dog responding to your touch. What better way for both of you to relax and enjoy each other's company?

Dental Care

To keep your dog's smile white and shining, keep him supplied with dental chew toys like sterile marrow bones, Nylabone® Chew and Brush, and floss. Feeding dry food and dog treats also helps keep plaque and tartar to a minimum. Clean his teeth once

Chewing is a necessary part of your dog's development and allows him the chance to explore his surroundings. Providing him with safe chew toys will keep his jaw occupied and prevent him from chewing on unacceptable objects..

a week with a gauze pad dipped in baking soda or doggie toothpaste. (People toothpaste will make him sick.) If you're hesitant or squeamish, your veterinarian can show you how.

9

Dog Training 101

· ·

One of the most important things you can do for your new
dog—and for your relationship—is to teach him some
simple lessons in obedience. He'll appreciate the time you're
spending together, and you'll appreciate having a well-behaved
dog in your life.

Some Basic Principles

A dog's first lesson must be that you're the one in charge. All
dogs learn by repetition.

■ You give a command once—you mean what you say.

■ Never give a command you can't reinforce or follow through.

■ Use short, crisp commands: "Quiet," "Down." "Easy." (Don't
  muck it up with lots of conversation, "Ginger, I told you to Sit
  and I mean it, for heaven's sake! SIT, will you please SIT!")

■ Put some oomph into your voice. If you say "No, no," but
  your voice says, "Please," your dog probably won't believe you
  or obey.

■ Firm does not mean nasty or angry.

■ Use a high-pitched happy voice during training sessions.

■ No hitting or yelling allowed. It could injure the dog and will set back his training as well as his attitude about the person he's trying to please (you).

■ Never call you dog to you to discipline him.

■ Be patient. Some dogs learn quickly, others take more time.

■ Be consistent. If you allow a behavior today (sitting on the sofa with you) but not tomorrow (when your sister visits), how will your dog ever know what you expect of him? The rules apply all the time.

■ Be positive. Believe your dog is smart and will learn his lessons well. He will sense your trust – that's what dogs do best.

Basic Commands Every Dog Should Know

Plan for you and your dog to attend a weekly obedience class to learn the best way to communicate with each other. It will be your night out together plus provide you with an incentive to work with your dog between classes so you'll be the best team there (and won't look foolish because you didn't practice!).

But don't wait for a training class to start teaching your dog good manners. Certain command words must become part of your dog's vocabulary if you're to live in peace and harmony together. Start your training in a quiet familiar place without distractions. As the dog becomes more proficient, more your sessions to different places like your driveway or a neighbor's yard (if you have good neighbors). Gradually add outside distractions during his session. A dog who sits in his own living room but not at the

One of the most important things you can do for your dog and your relationship with him is to provide him with basic training.

beach or park is not a trained or well-behaved dog.

Make training sessions short, five or ten minutes, even shorter lessons for a puppy. Work on one command at a time and repeat each command eight or ten times per session. Don't overdo it or you'll bore the dog. You can use a combination of food treats and verbal and hands-on praise to teach the meaning of each command. What works best with one dog won't motivate another.

The Release Word

Devise a release word so your dog will know when the training session ends or when you want him to take a break in between. "Break" or "Free" are in fact the words preferred; "Okay" is too common in our daily conversation and could confuse the dog. Don't use the dog's name when giving "Sit" and "Down"

Many dogs learn enthusiastically when given a food or treat reward for a job well done.

(stationary) commands, but do use his name in combination with moving commands such as "Let's Go" and "Come."

Start each workout with a leash and training collar on your dog. It's also helpful to exercise your dog a bit before you train. It will take the edge off his energy and boost his attention level.

The Sit Command

Food training works wonders with a pup, and many adult dogs learn more easily with food. Use tiny bits of puppy biscuit or slices of hot dog or cheese cut in half. Stand in front of the dog, hold the treat just above his nose, and move it slightly backwards over the top of his head—not too high or he'll stand on his rear feet to reach it. He should tilt backward for the food with his rear sliding toward the floor. Say the command, "Sit!" as you maneuver the food. As soon as the dog's rump hits the floor, praise him, "Good dog, Sit!" and give him the treat. When you dispense the food, use the other hand to scratch his ear as part of the hands-on praise. Eventually and intermittently, remove the food and praise with just your voice and hands. Do at least eight to ten repetitions at each session.

Be sure you praise while the dog is still sitting so he doesn't confuse praise with releasing from the Sit position. Puppies will take longer to master each command. Even though

It's important that your dog understands and performs the expected command before progressing to the next lesson.

they're usually eager students, there's a whole world full of goodies to investigate!

The Down Command

Puppies learn everything best with food. When teaching down, hold the bit of food to the dog's nose, tell him "Down," once, and lower the treat to the floor, pushing backwards toward the dog's front feet. Keep pushing the food backwards at floor level, and the dog should lower his body to the floor. The moment all four legs are down, tell him "Good dog, Down" and give the food. Rub his ears with

Get Off

Using the word "Off" instead of "Down" is less confusing to the dog when getting him off the furniture or dealing with jumping.

Hand signals can be used in conjunction with basic commands. This dog easily obeys his master's command for the down/stay.

your free hand at the same time. Once the dog has mastered Down and Sit, wait just a bit longer each time to give the food so he learns not to break position. That's the beginning of the Stay command.

The Stay Command

Once your dog responds well to sit and down, add the stay command by placing your hand out, palm facing the dog, and telling him to, "Stay." At first, just wait a few seconds, then release him and praise and reward. Gradually increase the time in ten-second increments as well as your distance from the dog. Remember, puppies have a very hard time with this command, so give him time and make training sessions very short.

Walking on a Leash

Before your dog will walk nicely, he has to be comfortable with the leash. Most dogs learn to love their leash because they know it means they are going out. But it's not uncommon at first for a dog to object violently and tug and pull in every direction except the right one. Start by attaching the leash to his buckle collar for a couple hours each day for two or three days and letting him get used to the feel of it.

When you start your walk together, tell your dog "Let's go," in a happy voice. Keep a treat in your hand and let the dog sniff it so he stays by your side. Walk around your yard or driveway, move ahead briskly and chat with him as you go, "Okay, good boy!"

Keep the leash loose with a little slack in it. When he moves too far ahead, tell him "Easy," and stop. If he lags or dawdles, repeat, "Let's go," and lure him with the treat.

If he's doing well, walk for a minute or two, then stop and give him the treat and a good hug. Repeat the process for three or four times. He won't really understand this walking business until he's got the hang of it. If he fights or struggles with the leash, limit walking to 10 or 12 successful paces, then take a "Good Dog!" Increase the walking distance as your dog improves.

The Come Command

Coming to you should be the happiest thing your dog ever does. Keep that thought uppermost whenever you tell your dog to "Come."

You can start teaching it as a separate command while teaching the ones we've just discussed. Attach a 10- or 12-foot lead or lightweight long line to his collar. Hold the other end and call him to you using his name and "Come." If he doesn't come immediately, tug and reel him in to you as you turn and run backwards so he thinks it's a game. Face the dog when he reaches you, tell him he's fabulous and give him a treat along with a hug. Acting like a silly fool will enhance the game. (Repeat – this is important – coming to mom or dad should always be his favorite thing to do.)

As with earlier commands, say "Come" only once so he doesn't think it's a three- or four-word command. Start by calling your dog only when you're sure he will respond. It's important to make every call a big success. Be creative and set up situation so you're sure your pal will come.

Gradually work at greater distances using a longer line of 20 to 30 feet. Now wait until the dog is distracted, call his name with the command and a tug on the rope if he doesn't come at once. Continue with intermittent food rewards until he's totally reliable. You never eliminate the verbal and hands-on praise, that's your lifelong gift to him.

Mixed breeds can participate in certain events, such as agility. However, even if you don't plan for your mixed breed to compete, the benefits of basic training will make him a valued member of the community.

Until your dog is totally reliable, coming when he's called, just keep that 20-foot line on him whenever he's outdoors. The dog won't mind a bit, and you'll have that all-important control you need. It's not uncommon for puppies to wear a long line until they're one year old.

The cardinal rule of the come command is to never discipline or scold a dog when he comes to you. That's the quickest way to turn "Come" into "Go Away Fast." The dog will associate coming to you with the punishment, not with running away, sniffing about or whatever he did (or your thought he did) wrong. Then he won't want to come anymore, and can you blame him? You also shouldn't call your dog to come for anything he might find unpleasant, like baths or giving medication—go and get him instead.

Thinking Ahead

Once you've mastered the basic obedience skills, you can begin to think about future training. However, don't lose sight of what training is all about—good behavior and respect for each other. Remember, your dog is not the only one being trained—you are, too.

Canine Good Citizen Test

Every dog should be a good canine citizen, and now the American Kennel Club offers a certificate to prove it. In 1989, the AKC established an educational

With the proper guidance and training, your unique adopted dog can excel in anything, whether it is the Canine Good Citizen test, therapy work, or as a loving companion.

program to encourage dog owners to teach their dogs to be model citizens. Well-behaved canine neighbors promote responsible dog ownership and are potent weapons against the anti-dog forces that threaten our rights as dog owners. Available to mixed-breed as well as purebred dogs, the CGC program awards certificates to dogs who pass this ten-step test:

- Accepting a friendly stranger: The dog must not appear shy or resentful when the evaluator approaches and greets the owner.

- Sit politely for petting: The dog must sit quietly while the evaluator approaches and pets him.

- Appearance and grooming: The evaluator greets and speaks to the dog, handles him gently, and checks him for health and hygiene.

- Walking on a loose lead: The dog must walk easily at your side without tugging or revisiting and without restraint from a tight lead.

- Walking through a crowd: The dog must weave with you through a group of three or four people without evidence of shyness or aggression.

- Sit and down on command/staying in place: The dog must obey these commands, although you may give them more than once.

- Come when called: You walk 10 feet from the dog, turn to face the dog and then call him to you. The dog may be left in the sit, down, or standing position. You may use body language or encouragement when calling the dog.

- Reaction to another dog: You and your dog walk past another person and his dog, and you shake hands with the person without your dog showing aggression or shyness. You may command your dog to stay.

■ Reaction to distractions: As you walk your dog, a tester drops a book, slams a door, or performs another noisy activity. Your dog should not try to run away nor show extreme signs of fear or aggression.

■ Supervised separation: The dog is left alone on a leash with another person while you're out of sight. He should not bark, whine, howl or pace or register anything other than mild agitation or nervousness.

Most kennel and dog-training clubs hold regular CGC tests for the dog-owning community at large. It's fun and your dog gets a diploma you can be proud of. That's an extra-special accomplishment for an adopted dog!

Practice Canine Courtesty

Dog ownership requires certain courtesies. Your dog is part of the community, and you're responsible for how his presence affects your neighborhood. Your goal should be to make him welcome everywhere he might go.

In order to receive the Canine Good Citizen certificate, your dog must be able to sit politely for petting. This mixed breed has certainly passed the test.

■ Always clean up after your dog, whether in your own yard or in a public place. Plastic grocery bags make great poop scoopers to carry in your pocket.

- Keep your dog on a leash in public areas. Even a dog who responds well to verbal control can "lose it" once in a while and tear off after a squirrel or a rabbit.

- Teach your dog to accept friendly strangers, your neighbors, and the delivery people as explained in the CGC test. No one likes to be greeted by a noisy, snarling dog.

- Make your dog a good example and keep him clean and well groomed. You need to be as proud of him as he is of you.

- Take every precaution to ensure your dog doesn't damage your neighbor's property or garden. It will promote better friendship between you, greater respect for the dog, and better public relations within the community.

Good training will open up a whole new world to your adopted dog, and he will be welcomed everywhere you go.

10

Solving Problem Behaviors

· ·

Most dogs and their owners face the challenge of one or more behavioral problems: barking, jumping, chewing, etc. Adopted dogs will probably have one or more of these problems, as well as some problems specific to their situation, such as separation anxiety or submissive urination. Do not despair, with the three "Ps"—patience, persistence, and praise—most dogs can overcome their fears and be secure and well behaved in your household.

Separation Anxiety

Separation anxiety is caused when a dog is isolated from his owner or person he loves. It can also occur even if the dog thinks you might be leaving. He doesn't understand that you'll return, and he gets anxious, stressed, and fearful. It's no surprise then that separation anxiety is common among shelter dogs who think they're being abandoned once again. Typical reactions, ranging from mild to severe, include excessive barking, destructiveness, and inappropriate elimination.

Dr. Karen Overall at the Department of Clinical Studies, School of Veterinary Medicine, University of Pennsylvania,

To help your dog cope with separation, tone down your transitions and do not become overly emotional when you leave or return to your home.

found that canine attention-seeking behavior was a forerunner or milder version of separation anxiety. An emotionally needy dog that nudges you, sits on your foot, or obsessively follows you around may anticipate or "experience" your absence, even when you're there with him. She suggests curbing such dependence by spending time with your dog in daily activities such as running, brisk walks, games, and basic obedience, all of which will also build self-confidence in the dog. If that fails, gently distance yourself from your pet by completely ignoring all of his ardent overtures until he finally gets the point or just gets tired and stops. That's a tough order, since your natural instinct is to give extra love to your adopted dog. It may take days or weeks to curb separation anxiety, but stand your ground. Reward signs of independence calmly, not excitedly, to avoid reviving clinging behavior.

When you're with your dog, don't absentmindedly pet or fondle him. (He needs to earn this stuff, remember?) In many cases of separation anxiety, that constant attention only makes the stress worse when you're away and may even produce a more demanding animal when you're there.

Two recommended ways to cope with separation anxiety are desensitization and counterconditioning. Desensitizing (performing an action such as leaving home and returning in

Adopted dogs can become very bonded to their owners and may suffer anxiety when left alone.

small time increments so often your dog stops being upset by your departure) may eliminate separation barking, but it may take weeks to transform daily comings and goings into a non-issue.

To start, set aside some time each day. Begin with actions associated with leaving; hold your car keys, put on your hat, your usual "going out" gestures. Do them several times a day, but don't leave. Then leave and re-enter your house again and again. Remain out for varying intervals, at first very brief, then longer periods of time, staying within earshot to check if and when barking subsides. This may work better if you confine your dog away from the door in a crate or in a comfortable, disaster-proof area cornered off by a see-through barrier such as a baby gate or ex-pen. You can leave something that has your scent, an old tee shirt perhaps, for the dog to lie on. Leave a radio on while you're gone. Both music and talk show stations are good substitutes for your voice. Return as calmly as you left and avoid eye contact to maintain the "cool" atmosphere. No big hugs when you release the dog.

Counterconditioning, which can be used along with desensitization, consists of teaching your dog to associate your departure with a pleasant experience. Dr. Nicholas Dodman, director of the Behavior Clinic at Tufts University School of Veterinary Medicine, says a timed-release treat such as a sterile marrowbone stuffed with peanut butter is an effective distraction. A favorite biscuit given as the dog is being confined and a second one as you leave the house can work well.

Dodman recommends you provide stimulating doggie activities or treats when you can't be home with him. "Many zoo animals

Make sure that you spend enough quality time with your dog so that he gets the attention that he needs.

have to 'work' for their food, which zoo keepers deliberately hide in cracks, crevices, trees and even plastic containers," Dodman says. If your dog is a chow hound, try leaving a sustained-release food device – stuff a Rhino® with peanut butter or cheese spread or give him a Crazy Ball®, which releases treats when he plays with it. (Remember to reduce his daily ration by the amount he eats through these offerings—you don't want to sacrifice boredom for obesity.)

Dodman also suggests you provide "environmental enrichment" simply by giving your dog access to a windowsill so he can survey his "territory." That's assuming the dog is trustworthy enough to be left loose or uncrated.

Disciplinary tactics will not eliminate or diminish separation anxiety. In fact, it may harm your dog. Punishing a dog for something it can't control or has already done is pointless and cruel. The dog won't understand and will only become more stressed. When the dog displays symptoms of anxiety-driven behavior, give a "Sit-Stay" command, rewarding with treats and praise for the dog's compliance. Supplementing with such positive reinforcements can add to the success of your counter-conditioning program.

Chewing

Chewing is probably the most common canine behavior problem and, unfortunately, it's very normal canine behavior. Dogs, especially puppies, chew for a dozen reasons, all of them deeply ingrained through centuries of chewing ancestors. So, what's a human to do?

For starters, put your human things away where your dog or puppy can't get at them: No more dishtowels on the door handle, slippers on the bedroom floor, open bathroom doors (think toilet paper), or open wastebaskets. Your dog may actually tidy up your

Preventing your adopted puppy or dog from engaging in destructive behavior from the start will stop unacceptable behavior in the future.

house a bit! Then confine him to a safe spot void of any valuables when you can't watch him. Now give your dog his own chew objects, a few at a time. When you catch him chomping on your stuff, scold him with a firm "No," take it away and replace it with one of his own chewables, then praise him when he takes it. If her persistently returns to certain objects like your antique table legs, you can spray them with a bitter-tasting product to make them undesirable. Keep his toys in a container, preferable an indestructible one, where he can fetch them on his own.

Barking

Barking is second only to chewing in the annoyance department. Dogs bark for different reasons. If you have a barker, the first thing you need to ask yourself is: Why is he barking? If your neighbors complain that he is barking in the middle of the day while you are gone, try to find out a little more. He may be barking only when he hears the mail carrier and is warding off the approaching enemy, or he may bark each and every time he hears noises. He may be lonely and barking to make himself feel more confident. It may take a while to figure out, and you may have to observe your dog secretly, especially if he barks while you are gone.

The best way to stop excessive barking is to build your dog's confidence through basic training, exercise, time, and attention.

The best way to treat a barker is to build his confidence, which only comes through basic obedience, time, and attention. To start, leave the house as quietly as possible. Do not make a big fuss about saying goodbye to your puppy—it will only make him more anxious. Leave a radio or television on and be sure to exercise him before you go. A well-exercised dog is far more likely to sleep the day away while you are gone.

Do not reinforce your dog's barking by trying to quiet him with petting or praise. If your puppy barks in your presence, ignore him and give him a treat when he's quiet. If your puppy or dog barks when the doorbell rings, silently put him in another room. Give him attention only when he's quiet, and then have him perform an obedience command, like Sit or Down.

Although jumping up is most likely your dog's way of greeting you, it can be dangerous and should be prevented.

Jumping Up

Jumping up is not only natural behavior for a canine, it's been reinforced almost from birth. When puppies stand on their tiptoes and peek over the top of their whelping box, they get picked up and are rewarded with a hug or kiss. They jump on the baby gates to visit us and we instantly scoop them up. By eight or nine weeks of age, their jumping has produced only positive results; fortunately, it's not irreversible.

If you hope to teach your dog not to jump on you or other people, you have to be consistent. As in your basic dog rules, you can't overlook it today, then expect it never to occur again.

Dogs literally jump for joy – when you come home, when visitors arrive, when they're excited about what's happening. To be successful, you must insist that your friends and family also never allow or encourage the behavior.

The best correction is teaching alternate behavior. Make the dog "Sit-Stay" when you come him or your friends come to the door. Insist he stay, then praise him calmly while he's sitting so that sitting is rewarded. If he jumps up, use the "Off" command and replace him in the "Sit" position.

Avoid using traditional methods of correction, such as kneeing in the chest or stepping on his toes, which can inadvertently harm your dog. For a persistent jumper, try the paw-hold when he jumps. Simply grasp his front paws and stand there, don't release them. Eventually, he'll whine or try to pull away. Hang on a few more seconds, release and make him sit, then praise him because he sat. Easy to do, and it works!

Digging

Dogs dig for many reasons, all of them logical to the dog. Breed heritage motivates many dogs to dig; it's in there genes. Some need an outlet for extra energy, some dig out of loneliness or boredom, some just because it's fun.

Try to determine why your dog digs. If he digs to cool himself off in damp places, make sure he has adequate shade and water, provide him with a wading pool or house him in a cool area of the house. Is he digging to escape, and why? For companionship, excitement if he's bored, to mate if he's still intact? Those are all fixable problems. Your fence should fit tight to the ground or even be buried a few inches underneath so he can't burrow under it.

If all else fails, try giving him his own digging spot. When he digs anywhere else, tell him "No" and take him to his spot, then praise him when he digs there.

You should always be consistent with household rules; for example, if you do not want your dog to jump on the furniture, then make sure that rule is always obeyed.

If you are having difficulty training your dog, especially with biting or aggression, search for a professional trainer. A reputable dog trainer will be able to determine the most suitable training approach.

Obviously supervision is a must until his outdoor mischief is under control.

In dealing with digging or any other behavior problem, you should ask, "Am I maintaining quality time with regular play, exercise, and walks?" Dogs need attention and shared activities just like children do.

Nipping and Biting

Simply put, nipping and biting should not be allowed, not even playful nipping. If permitted or ignored, it will only escalate into more aggressive behavior. It's also easier and wiser to nip the nipping in the bud when puppy is 7 pounds instead of 70.

Play nipping can be discouraged by pulling your hand away and saying, "ouch!" Then turn your back or leave the room for 60 seconds, depriving puppy of your companionship.

If your adult dog growls, bites or curls his lips at you or other people, you should get professional advice. Discuss it with the shelter staff, your obedience instructor or consult an animal behaviorist—never risk a dog bite.

Friends for Life

You don't have to settle for a dog that misbehaves, and now you have some tools to help you get on track with your relationship with your adopted dog. Stock up on those 3 P's, always be consistent, and teach your adopted dog what he needs to know in order to get along in your family. If you tackle your problems now, you will have a wonderful companion.

It is hard work—training an adopted puppy or dog takes determination and effort, but the results are worth it. Just think of all the fun that you and your canine companion can have and your bright future together.

Resources

. . . .

Books

Adamson, Eve.
The Simple Guide to a Healthy Dog.
New Jersey: TFH Publications, 2002.

Allred, Alexandra Powe.
Teaching Basic Obedience: Train the Owner, Train the Dog.
New Jersey: TFH Publications, 2001.

Aloff, Brenda.
Positive Reinforcement: Training Dogs in the Real World.
New Jersey: TFH Publications, 2001.

Bauman, Diane.
Beyond Basic Dog Training, new, updated edition.
New York: Howell Book House, 1991.

Becker, Dr. Marty.
The Healing Power of Pets.
New York: Hyperion, 2002.

Bonham, Margaret.
The Simple Guide to Getting Active with Your Dog.
New Jersey: TFH Publications, 2001.

Coile, D. Caroline, Ph.D.
Encyclopedia of Dog Breeds.
New York: Barron's Educational Series, 1998.

DePrisco, Andrew and Johnson, James.
Choosing a Dog for Life
New Jersey, TFH Publications, 1996.

Dunbar, Dr. Ian
Before You Get Your Puppy.
California: James & Kenneth Publishers, 2001.

Kennedy, Stacy.
The Simple Guide to Puppies.
New Jersey: TFH Publications, 2000.

Palika, Liz.
All Dogs Need Some Training.
New York: Howell Book House, 1997

Pitcairn, Richard, DVM, and Susan Hubble Pitcairn.
Dr. Pitcairn's Guide to Natural Health for Dogs and Cats.
Pennsylvania: Rodale Press, 1995.

Pryor, Karen.
Don't Shoot the Dog! The New Art of Teaching and Training.
New York: Bantam Books, 1984.

Volhard, Jack and Wendy.
The Canine Good Citizen: Every Dog Can Be One.
New York: Howell Book House, 1997.

Volhard, Wendy and Kerry Brown, DVM.
Holistic Guide for a Healthy Dog, second edition.
New York: Howell Book House, 2000.

Wood, Deborah.
Help for Your Shy Dog.
New York: Howell Book House, 1999.

Periodicals

ASPCA Animal Watch
315 East 62nd Street
New York, NY 10021
www.aspca.org

Dog & Kennel
Pet Publishing, Inc.
7-L Dundas Circle
Greensboro, NC 27407

Organizations

American Kennel Club
Headquarters:
260 Madison Avenue
New York, NY 10016
Operations Center:
5580 Centerview Drive
Raleigh, NC 27606-3390
Customer Service:
Phone: (919) 233-9767
www.akc.org

American Kennel Club's Canine Good Citizen
www.akc.org/love/cgc/index.cfm

American Kennel Club's National Breed Club Rescue
www.akc.org/breeds/rescue.cfm

American Mixed Breed Obedience Association
179 Niblick Road #113
Paso Robles, CA 93446
Phone: (805) 226-9275
www.amborusa.org

Animal Behavior Society
Indiana University
2611 East 10th Street #170
Bloomington, IN 47408-2603
www.animalbehavior.org

Association of Companion Animal Behavior Counselors
C/o American Instiute for Animla Science
PO Box 7922
Rego Park, NY 11374-7922
www.animalbehaviorcounselors.org

Association of Pet Dog Trainers
17000 Commerce Parkway, Suite C
Mt. Laurel, NJ 08054
Phone: 1-800-PET-DOGS
www.apdt.com

The Canadian Kennel Club
89 Skyway Avenue, Suite 100
Etobicoke, Ontario, Canada
M9W 6R4
Order Desk & Membership: 1-800-250-8040
Fax: (416) 675-6506
www.ckc.ca

Humane Society of the United States
2100 L St., NW
Washington, DC 20037
www.hsus.org

The Kennel Club
1 Clarges Street
London
W1J 8AB
Phone: 087 0606 6750
Fax: 020 7518 1058
www.the-kennel-club.org.uk

North American Dog Agility Council
11522 South Hwy 3
Cataldo, ID 83810
www.nadac.com

North Shore Animal League
750 Port Washington Blvd.
Port Washington, NY 11050
Phone: (516) 883-7900
www.nsalamerica.org

Therapy Dogs International, Inc.
88 Bartley Road
Flanders, NJ 07836
www.tdi-dog.org

The United Kennel Club, Inc.
100 E. Kilgore Road
Kalamazoo, MI 49002-5584
Phone: (616) 343-9020
www.ukcdogs.com

United States Dog Agility Association (USDAA)
PO Box 850955
Richardson, TX 75085-0955
Phone: (972) 231-9700
Information Line: (888) AGILITY
www.usdaa.com

Websites

Dog Agility
www.dogpatch.org/agility

Dog Bite Law Information
www.dogbitelaw.com

Dog FAQ
www.k9web.com/dog-faqs/

Dog Obedience and Training
www.dogpatch.org/obed/

Dog Watch
www.dogwatch.net/links.html

Flyball
www.flyballdogs.com/
www.flyball.org/home.htm

I-Love-Dogs.com
www.i-love-dogs.com/

International Association of Canine Professionals
www.dogpro.org/

International Weight Pull Association
www.eskimo.com/~samoyed/iwpa/

Index

· · · · · · · · · · · · · · · · · · · ·

Adopting a Great Dog